Barack Obama
Eight Years

Contents

Bring this TIME Special Edition to life in 60 seconds or less:

1) Download the free TIME Special Edition App
2) Select "Experience"
3) Point the camera of your phone or tablet at the cover image or at any of the three designated augmented-reality-experience photos, found on pages 43, 53 and 96
4) Enjoy the audio- and video-enhanced AR experience

A PRESIDENT BUILDS HIS IDENTITY

From his first day in office, Barack Obama was a different kind of commander in chief

The acceptance speech, Democratic National Convention, Denver, Aug. 28, 2008

The president comes home, through the White House's South Portico, after a day of speaking in Vermont and Maine in 2012.

President Obama and First Lady Michelle Obama in the inaugural parade, Pennsylvania Avenue, Jan. 21, 2013

SEAL OF THE PRESIDENT OF THE
STATES

President Obama is greeted by lawmakers after his last State of the Union address, Jan. 12, 2016.

HONOR AND EFFORT

He revived the economy and reoriented foreign policy. His promise of "hope and change" proved harder to deliver

By David Von Drehle

Barack Obama entered the White House as something new in American history. He wasn't chosen on the basis of experience, nor for his role as leader of a party or a movement. He had not been a governor or a general or a veteran legislator. He did not become president by the accident of his predecessor's death in office.

Obama was elected purely for himself—his message, his persona and what he symbolized. In 48 brief months, he rose from the obscurity of a state legislature to become the first Democrat in more than three decades to win more than half of the popular vote. Messenger and message were inseparable; he offered himself as Exhibit A in the case for hope and change. Obama was a mirror in which millions of people saw their cherished ideals reflected: tolerance, cooperation, equality, justice.

After two bruising and tumultuous terms in office—a period of economic crisis and geopolitical upheaval—it's difficult to recall how the young candidate riveted the world simply by being Obama. As a mere nominee, not yet elected, he drew an estimated crowd of 200,000 people—in Germany. He filled a football stadium for his acceptance speech, a city park for his victory speech and, of course,

Workers install Shepard Fairey's campaign-poster portrait of Barack Obama at the National Portrait Gallery in 2009.

New Arrivals

President Obama answers questions during a health-care town hall meeting in Cleveland, above; opposite page, the president fist-bumps custodian Lawrence Lipscomb in 2009.

much of the National Mall for his first inauguration. In October 2009, the Nobel Prize committee awarded him its most prestigious honor, the Peace Prize, before he'd had time to accomplish much at all. "Only very rarely has a person to the same extent as Obama captured the world's attention and given its people hope for a better future," the prize citation declared. A Nobel Peace Prize just for being Obama.

In a sense, there was nowhere to go but down. The most exalted position in American life has a way of humbling its occupants. Obama leaves office more human than he entered it, a mere mortal with a track record and the gray hair to show for it. And that track record contains much more than his enemies—or even many of his friends—have been ready to acknowledge.

Taking office in the midst of an economic meltdown, Obama seized on the massive federal response to make record investments in education initiatives, environmental research, industrial modernization and, most famously, health-care reform. He poured money into basic medical and scientific research and supercharged the U.S. alternative-energy sector. His high-stakes reorientation of American foreign policy worries many experts, and the results might not be fully understood for years. But the effort cannot be called small.

Indeed, Obama's record is bigger and more substantial than even he allowed himself to admit through much of his time in office. A candidate known for his stirring speeches struggled, as president, to sell the public on what he was doing and why he was doing it.

Journalist Michael Grunwald has documented the scope of one of Obama's ambitious achievements: the stimulus package known as the American Recovery and Reinvestment Act. In constant dollars, the ARRA was "more than 50 percent bigger than the entire New Deal, twice as big as the Louisiana Purchase and Marshall Plans combined," Grunwald wrote in his 2012 book, *The New New Deal: The Hidden Story of Change in the*

Obama Era. It was "the biggest . . . education reform bill since the Great Society," he continued. The "biggest foray into industrial policy since FDR, biggest expansion of antipoverty initiatives since Lyndon Johnson, biggest middle-class tax cut since Ronald Reagan, biggest infusion of research money ever." And that was just one of several massive Obama undertakings. He stormed into the banking, automotive and health-care industries, winning changes that had been mulled, debated and dithered over for decades.

Yet the president was often downbeat—seemingly discouraged—about the impact he was having. He complained loudly and often of the obstructions put in his path by his Republican opponents. "The American people may have voted for divided government, but they didn't vote for a dysfunctional government," Obama said after the GOP captured the House of Representatives in 2010. Voters could be forgiven if they concluded that Obama must not be getting much done.

It was as if Obama had fallen under his own spell and began measuring himself not by real wins in the political trenches but by the ephemeral goals of his soaring speeches. "This is our moment," Obama had said on the night he won the election. "This is our time to put our people back to work and open doors of opportunity for our kids; to restore prosperity and promote the cause of peace; to reclaim the American dream and reaffirm that fundamental truth that, out of many, we are one." At points in his presidency, Obama couldn't hide his disappointment that his every dream had not come true.

Through eight years in office, Barack Obama used all the tools in a president's kit to make significant changes: laws, rules, executive orders and the bully pulpit. Yet he couldn't change the nature of politics itself. The irony of Obama's presidency is that he achieved more than most presidents—yet millions of Americans grew convinced during his administration that Washington can't get anything done.

THE WORLD ECONOMY WAS PLUNGING LIKE a runaway bobsled as Obama took the oath of office in January 2009 before one of the largest gatherings in the history of the nation's capital.

After a steep run-up in housing prices in the U.S. and elsewhere, the bursting bubble sent millions of homes into foreclosure. This mortgage crisis in turn blazed through the global banking system, and only an extraordinary intervention by lame-duck president George W. Bush prevented a complete financial collapse.

Obama inherited the wreckage of what proved to be the worst U.S. recession since the 1930s. The economy contracted by more than 8%. Unemployment doubled, from 5% to 10%—a net loss of some 8 million jobs. Average housing prices dropped by 30%. The cumulative wealth of Americans fell by nearly a quarter: a loss on paper of some $15 trillion. As the Great Recession echoed around the world, Europe's economy went into reverse. Nations from Greece to Iceland flirted with default on their sovereign debts, while emerging markets from Rio to New Delhi and Moscow to Beijing began to sputter and stall.

Having campaigned on "the audacity of hope," Obama was thrust into a contagion of fear. Fear of lending froze capital markets; fear of investment idled assembly lines and sent stock exchanges tumbling. And fear that something even worse might lie ahead caused consumers to hunker down and stop spending.

Obama's new administration went immediately to work on the largest economic-stimulus bill ever enacted by Congress—about $800 billion. Much of the money went to tax relief, unemployment insurance and other direct infusions of cash into the pockets of Americans who would, in turn, the administration hoped, spend or invest it. But the new president also seized the chance to pump billions into priorities that would normally struggle to receive much smaller sums. The stimulus bill was packed with record spending on renewable energy, a modern electrical grid, computerization of health-care records, high-speed rail, and new bridges and roads. Obama also directed billions to basic scientific research, hoping to sow seeds of discovery that would yield the next wave of American innovation.

"From the National Institutes of Health to the National Science Foundation, this recovery act represents the biggest increase in basic research funding in the long history of America's noble endeavor to better understand our world," Obama told an audience in Denver less than a month after taking the oath. "And just as President Kennedy sparked an explosion of innovation when he set America's sights on the moon, I hope this investment will ignite our imagination once more, spurring new discoveries and breakthroughs in science, in medicine, in energy, to make our economy stronger and our nation more secure and our planet safer for our children."

The extent of the economic emergency al-

President Obama is known for keeping late hours. Here, he works in the Oval Office at the Resolute desk, which was a gift from Queen Victoria to President Rutherford B. Hayes in 1880.

lowed Obama to fulfill a catalog of campaign promises in the first dizzy weeks of his administration—that is, to make good on pledges he made to invest. According to the Congressional Budget Office, the recovery act boosted growth in the U.S. by 1% to 4% in 2010, with smaller impacts in subsequent years. That's not bad by historical standards, but Obama was reluctant to boast; it was not the rapid repair that he had envisioned, and it was hardly enough to cure such a deep recession.

So it was that the unprecedented bill drew harsh criticism from both ends of the political spectrum: conservatives called it a wasteful "porkulus," while liberals complained that it was too small to be effective. Though there has been a clear positive influence, Obama's advisers were not going to brag about the bill while millions of Americans were out of work—and besides, there wasn't much time for bragging, because the president was rushing ahead into other crises.

The auto industry was facing disaster. At the onset of the crisis in October 2007, sales of cars and light trucks had been humming at about 16 million per year. But over the end stretch of the Bush administration, that production plummeted. By the end of February 2009, with Obama fewer than 50 days into the job, that number was down to 9 million, a year-over-year drop of more than 40%. Two of the Big Three U.S. automakers—General Motors and Chrysler—teetered on the brink of bankruptcy, with Ford at risk of being dragged down with them. The entire auto supply chain, with millions of workers at countless companies across the country, was at risk.

Obama moved forcefully to shore up the industry. But rather than dole out tax dollars while asking little in return, he wielded the bailout funds to force rapid streamlining and reforms, such as having fewer dealerships and more flexible pay scales. Critics, appalled at what they felt was federal overreach, gave GM a new name: "Government Motors."

AMERICANS ENDED UP WITH A STRONGER FINANCIAL SYSTEM AND GOT THEIR MONEY BACK.

Government is not an economics seminar, however—it's the real world. Obama could see all the jobs at stake, and he pictured the families and communities behind those jobs. Initial estimates of the bailout price tag exceeded $80 billion, but as the bank industry recovered, taxpayers recovered all of the money Obama pumped into it and almost all of what went to Detroit. By 2015, American car and truck makers were banking record profits on booming sales—at little cost to taxpayers.

During those panicked early months, Obama was also pressing ahead with the unpopular bailout of the banking industry that began under President Bush. By most measures, it worked: instead of a cascade of bank failures, Americans ended up with a stronger financial system, and the public got its money back. All the tax dollars devoted to the bank rescue wound up being repaid.

But that didn't matter much to the public. Millions of Americans came to the conclusion that reckless Wall Streeters caused the financial crisis—and skated past the consequences thanks to political connections. Beginning with the Tea Party movement of 2010, populist candidates on both the right and the left fed on this widespread anger. Republican Donald Trump spoke ominously of a "rigged" system. In Obama's own party, Sen. Bernie Sanders stirred up a fire from the embers of resentment. Though Obama spent the rest of his presidency tightening banking regulations, he never managed to shake off these critics.

AND THEN THERE IS "OBAMACARE," THE president's hugely ambitious, yet troubled, health-care reform. Rammed through Congress without a single Republican vote, the Affordable Care Act is Obama's attempt to deliver on a promise that Democrats have made for generations: medical insurance for all. At the same time, the law is an unprecedented effort to break the fever of runaway medical costs.

The future of Obamacare is uncertain, and President-elect Donald Trump has expressed disdain for the act. The private-insurance exchanges at the heart of the plan appear to be at risk. Although millions of Americans have gained coverage, too many of those are among the chronically ill, and too few are young and healthy. The result: more claims and less revenue than projected, leading to higher premiums. Fears of a so-called death spiral, in which rising premiums drive off all but the sickest customers, have some Democrats once again calling for a government takeover, something opponents label "socialized medicine."

But while that old argument heats up again, other provisions of Obamacare are spurring a revolution. Through a combination of carrots and sticks, the law has raised the proportion of doctors and hospitals using electronic medical records from about 1 in 5 to more than 4 in 5. Though this transition can be rocky, experts continue to believe that computerized records will work data-driven miracles, greatly reducing medical errors, cutting useless or redundant treatments, and steering health-care providers to the best approaches.

In other words, Obamacare is a work in progress. And this points to something im-

Bo, one of the Obama family's Portuguese water dogs, looks up as the president walks through the Oval Office doors in 2013.

portant about the presidency: it always has the ring of unfinished business. No president, whether having served for many years or a partial term, has stepped away with his work complete, nor without some baggage left behind in the Oval Office. The presidency is a relay race with no known finish line, and America's challenges and opportunities persist through each passing of the baton. Questions and issues—like the problem of affordable health care—will continue to evolve long after Obama's tenure is done.

STILL, OBAMA CARRIED THE BATON A GREAT distance, and he leaves America in a different place than he found it. Here are a few more of the many examples:

Private lenders no longer dominate the college-student-loan business. By making loans directly, rather than providing guarantees for private loans, government has transferred billions of dollars that used to pay lenders into new loans at cheaper rates.

Obama doubled the number of female justices in Supreme Court history, from two to four, and appointed the first justice of Hispanic heritage, Sonia Sotomayor.

Same-sex couples are free to wed, in part because Obama's Department of Justice refused to support the so-called Defense of Marriage Act. Gays serve openly in the military because Obama ended "don't ask, don't tell." Women can choose to qualify for combat roles.

Greenhouse-gas emissions are down some 12% in the U.S., and the White House projects even steeper drops over the next decade, thanks to massive investments in more-efficient appliances, buildings, cars, trucks and power lines. America is generating more energy from renewable sources and less from coal. Meanwhile, Obama has deflected efforts from inside his own party to halt the fracking revolution—a technological win-win that has cut carbon dioxide emissions while freeing the U.S. from dependence on foreign oil.

When it comes to foreign policy, only time will reveal whether the baton Obama passes is stuffed with TNT. His opening to Cuba seemed overdue, given the collapse of Castroism in the shattered economies of Havana and Caracas. His cautious approach to China kept

Obama and Vice President Joe Biden head for lunch in a White House private dining room, 2011.

relations with the rising power steady even as Beijing struggled with economic growing pains. In fact, by some measures Obama leaves the U.S. in a stronger position in Asia and the Pacific than it was the day he took office.

But what about the Middle East? Obama delivered on his promise to get American troops out of Iraq, and he greatly limited U.S. involvement in Afghanistan. But history is likely to judge him by the outcome of his high-stakes bet on Iran. A best-case scenario: five or 10 or 20 years from now, pragmatic leaders will have come to power from Tehran to Ankara, from Cairo to Riyadh, tempering the Sunni-Shia conflict in favor of regional peace. Obama leans this way because he is a big believer in pragmatism—maybe too big. Because the worst-case scenario is a regional conflagration in which the Shia mullahs of Iran and the Sunni sheiks of Saudi Arabia pile a nuclear-arms race atop their centuries-old religious rivalry.

EIGHT YEARS AFTER OBAMA TOOK OFFICE with the economy crashing around his ears, people are still arguing about his accomplishments. What matters more: the stubbornly low growth that makes this the slowest recovery on record, or the longest string of consecutive job gains in recorded history? The U.S. economy is nearly $1 trillion bigger today than it was before the crisis, and most other developed countries have fared worse.

Such debates are good. They are the stuff of history and the currency of a free society, and Obama's impact will be discussed and reexamined for years.

Yet there is something that seems unassailable, and it goes a long way toward explaining the steady rise in the president's approval ratings as Americans contemplate his last day at the helm. Despite his inexperience, Barack Obama gave a full measure of scandal-free service, a rarity among modern presidents. And he never lost hope, even when others wavered. There is no tougher job—an endless stream of difficult decisions, all guaranteed to stir fierce criticism. Obama did it with dignity and conscience. As was true at the beginning, it remains true at the end: who Obama was mattered at least as much as what he did. And start to finish, he was an honorable man.

CHAPTER ONE

A DISTINCTIVE AGENDA

“Change will not come if we wait for some other person or if we wait for some other time. We are the ones we’ve been waiting for. We are the change that we seek.”

—Barack Obama, 2008 campaign

BAILING OUT THE ECONOMY

Obama took office in the midst of a financial calamity. Then things started to turn around

By Philip Elliott

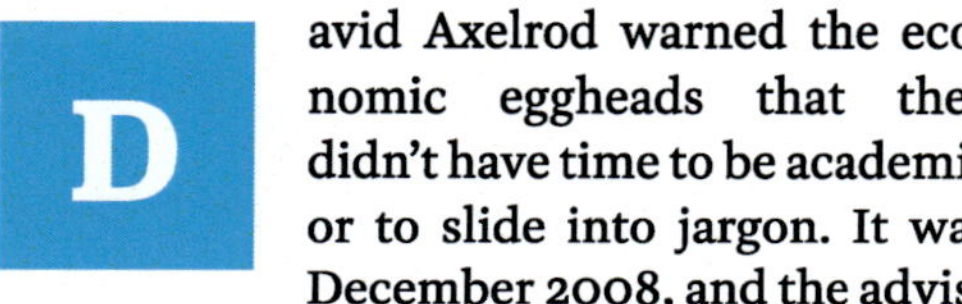

David Axelrod warned the economic eggheads that they didn't have time to be academic or to slide into jargon. It was December 2008, and the advisers, part of Barack Obama's transition team, were scheduled to meet the president-elect later in the day. The briefing could leave no doubt about the problems their boss would inherit in a few short weeks, said Axelrod, Obama's veteran communications strategist. It had to be a "holy-s--- moment." Berkeley economist Christina Romer, joining the cabinet as its chief economic adviser, flushed as she used that exact phrase in her presentation. The president-elect, confronted with her bleak 57-page memo and salty language, chuckled. It was the lone moment of levity.

Obama knew the economy was in trouble. He had cited the nation's financial woes unrelentingly during his campaign to attack rival John McCain—and most Republicans, really—as irresponsible. But it was during the briefing, at which his team spelled out what was melting down and, in an 11-page appendix, what could be done to reverse course, that Obama began to grasp the daunting task ahead. "This economy is in bad shape. And we have just completed one of the longest election cycles in recorded history," Obama said during his transition to power. "Now is a good time for us to set politics aside for a while and think practically about what will actually work to move the economy forward."

Every president faces early challenges. George W. Bush confronted a standoff with China on his first days in power, and 9/11 followed just months later. Bill Clinton was on the job roughly a month when Osama bin Laden tried for the first time to take down the World Trade Center. Soon after, Clinton was battling a revolt from his own party on trade. George H.W. Bush was thrown by an economic downturn, and Ronald Reagan was tasked with bucking up a nation down on itself after the presidencies of Gerald Ford and Jimmy Carter.

But the financial calamity handed to Obama in January 2009 rivaled the Great Depression. Home loans, retirement funds, factory orders, food prices, college aid—everything seemed roiled by the fast-moving meltdown and its aftermath. When Obama took office, the economy was in a free fall, hemorrhaging an average of 738,000 jobs each month. Any and all solutions were fraught with political risk: the Republicans were vowing to ob-

President Obama at the Alcoa Davenport Works aluminum plant in Bettendorf, Iowa, 2011

ZONE 2

struct Obama's every move, and Democrats in charge of both chambers of Congress could be more hardheaded than members of the GOP.

The 44th president knew that no issue was more important to Americans than the economy. A family might fret about national security, global prestige and terrorism, but if the mortgage couldn't be paid, nothing else really mattered. Obama had to keep his focus at home. At least for a while, he needed his new secretary of state, Hillary Clinton, to go it alone. "You know, we've got this major economic crisis that may push us into a depression," Obama said, as Clinton would relate later. "I'm not going to be able to do a lot to satisfy the built-up expectations for our role around the world. So you're going to have to get out there and, you know, really represent us while I deal with, you know, the economic catastrophe I inherited."

Moving forward meant making a lot of difficult choices. Obama campaigned in broad brushstrokes of hope and arrived in office facing buckets of despair. During his first term, he chose to bail out automakers General Motors and Chrysler—but not Detroit itself. He poured taxpayer dollars into programs that installed solar panels, subsidized new cars, hired teachers and built bridges—but was

The president at a Ford assembly plant in Chicago in 2010; speaking about Wall Street while traders work on the New York Stock Exchange in 2010; and meeting with advisers about the economy in 2011

criticized by liberals for not going far enough. He extended unemployment benefits for Americans still stung by the global economic meltdown—but did not pursue criminal charges for those behind the crash.

"I found that in the very depths of the financial crisis, the cabinet and the advisers would be arguing about some pretty heavy stuff, and it was a scary moment when things could have gone terribly wrong," said Austan Goolsbee, who succeeded Romer as chair of the Council of Economic Advisers. "And I remember thinking many times, 'Thank God he's the one that has to decide this thing and not us.'"

NO PRESIDENT, OF COURSE, CAN SINGLE-handedly repair—or, for that matter, tank—a global financial system. It wasn't as if Obama alone had his hands on the economy's rudder or could even move it had he wanted to. Presidents cannot wave a wand and make restaurants add new waiters, cause Silicon Valley innovators' apps to suddenly take off or force

Fortune 500 C-suite executives to double department sizes. Broader factors come into play, including consumer confidence and the Federal Reserve's choices about where to keep lending rates. It is all interconnected, and Obama's initial goal was to keep money moving at every level.

A gifted speaker, a powerful political organizer and a constitutional-law professor, Obama was, however, no economist. To master the arcana, or at least better understand it, he assembled an economics squad to brief him regularly about financial risks, just as the intelligence community offered information about security threats. He leaned on Secretary of the Treasury Timothy Geithner and on Larry Summers, his in-house economic quarterback and head of the National Economic Council. In the early days, Summers emerged as the Oval Office's de facto economics professor, correcting anyone who had details wrong—including the president.

Humility went a long way, and Obama invited business leaders, historians, innovators and rule breakers to the White House for brainstorming sessions. Corporate CEOs ran into one another in the hallways, the residence became a salon for the smartest thinkers, and Obama's young campaign aides were dispatched to auto plants' parking lots to see firsthand what the administration was facing. The president's political team counseled him to be careful, and his economic team offered him similar advice. (When the chairmanship of the Federal Reserve was up during Obama's first term, he took the conservative route, renominating Ben Bernanke instead of putting forward his trusted guru, Summers. Change, at that point, could have sent the wrong signal to the financial community; he played it safe.)

One of President Obama's early victories was pushing Congress to pass an estimated $800 million stimulus-spending bill, known as the American Recovery and Reinvestment Act. The measure, which Obama had discussed as president-elect, aimed to "save or create" 3.5 million jobs by building infrastructure, offering tax cuts and investing in communities. Among other things, the act increased grants for college students, boosted teachers' salaries and shored up states struggling with falling revenues.

But not everything went as planned. The stimulus fell short of its goals and left segments of the public skeptical. Similarly, a much-lauded $80 billion clean-technology program, meant to create jobs and cut reliance on foreign oil, misfired when one ben-

THE INDICATORS

President Obama entered the White House during the worst financial crisis in the U.S. since the Great Depression and is credited with getting the economy back on course, reviving the job market and restoring consumer confidence. Yet wages under his watch stayed flat, and the federal debt reached historic highs. What do the numbers say about Obama's performance? Here's a snapshot. **By Emily Barone**

Unemployment

During the recession, unemployment peaked at 10%. But by late 2015 it had fallen to 5%—on par with pre-recession levels—and has hovered there ever since.

7.8%

January 2009

10% Peak rate under Obama

4.9%

October 2016

Government Spending

The federal government has covered its yearly expenses just five times in the past 50 years—in 1969 and from 1998 to 2001. Each year that the U.S. overspends, the amount is added to the running total of federal debt.

8-year budget balance
(2-term presidents)

Ronald Reagan	–$1.4 trillion
Bill Clinton	+$63 billion
George W. Bush	–$3.4 trillion
Barack Obama	–$6.4 trillion

Federal Debt

The debt, below, is best expressed as a percentage of GDP. Today that ratio is higher than it's been since World War II. Under Obama, the debt increased $8.7 trillion, due in part to the stimulus bill.

That's a 78% increase in 8 years

November 2016

$19,790,136,330,003.19

Housing

Obama passed a series of measures including a mortgage-refinancing program and a first-time-homebuyer tax credit, which, combined with low interest rates, helped to stabilize the housing market.

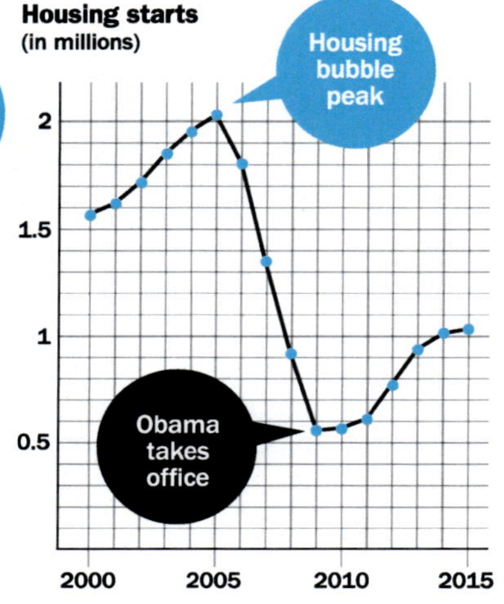

Household Debt

Since 2008, Americans have shed a trillion dollars in mortgage debt, while student-loan debt has more than doubled.

Types of household debt
(in trillions)

	2008		2016
Mortgage	9.3	→	8.4
Student loans	0.6	→	1.3
Auto loans	0.8	→	1.1

Stock Market

The Dow Jones Industrial Average increased 130% during the years Obama was in office.

7,949.09	18,249.36
Jan. 20, 2009	Nov. 7, 2016

Consumer Confidence

As employment increased, so did consumer confidence, which in turn helped buoy retail sales, which grew 35%.

Retail sales (YTD over past 8 years)

↑ **26%** Clothing

↑ **5%** Electronics and appliances

↑ **25%** Furniture

↑ **76%** New cars

↑ **16%** Sporting goods, books, music and hobbies

↑ **44%** Eating and drinking out

Big Business

The country's largest corporations have rebounded during the Obama administration, largely by slashing labor costs. In 2009, Fortune 500 companies dropped 821,000 jobs—more than 3% of their payroll.

Fortune 500 company profits

2009 **$391 billion**

2015 **$840 billion**

SOURCES: BLS; census; the White House; Nation Retail Federation; Yahoo Finance; *Fortune*; New York Fed Consumer Credit Panel/Equifax; Federal Reserve Bank of St. Louis; GAO; OMB; U.S. Treasury.
NOTES: Each president's budget balance is the sum of each of their eight years, starting with their first full fiscal year in office. Obama's first full fiscal year started in October 2009. His eight-year budget figure shown here includes the estimated deficit for the fiscal year 2017, which began in October 2016. Debt figures are based on the calendar years that each president was in office. Statistics are as of Nov. 7, 2016.

eficiary, the solar-panel company Solyndra, defaulted on a $535 million loan guaranteed by the Department of Energy. Republicans, embroiled in their own intraparty fights and Tea Party revolt, offered little help.

By the start of Obama's second term, however, the White House's economic maneuvering not only stopped the bleeding but appeared to jump-start the economy, returning it to levels last seen in the 1990s. The Federal Reserve did its part by keeping interest rates at nearly zero for almost eight years. (Nothing like almost-free cash to keep the economy humming.) The stock market reached record highs. Government spending grew at the lowest rate since Dwight Eisenhower's presidency. During his two administrations, Obama presided over 74 consecutive months of job growth—a streak that was interrupted in May 2016 only when 40,000 striking Verizon workers were counted as jobs lost. Even so, a full 15 million jobs appeared under his watch. Today, 95% of Americans are paying record-low federal income taxes.

THE U.S. OUTPACED OTHER COUNTRIES' ECONOMIC RECOVERIES, GROWING BY MORE THAN 10%.

And there was more. Under Obama, the U.S. outpaced other countries' economic recoveries, growing by more than 10% between the first quarter of 2008 and June 2016, while European nations ticked up just 0.64%, according to the Organization for Economic Co-operation and Development, which tracks global trends. Unemployment is on track to be under 5% when Obama exits the White House, down from the 10% he faced in his first term. In September 2016, the U.S. Census Bureau found that household income jumped 5% in 2015, the biggest gain on record. The Wall Street bailout, initiated by Obama's predecessor but executed under him, actually made the Treasury money. The deficit declined by roughly three quarters, or a cool $1 trillion, though it is expected to climb in coming years because of the aging population (more Social Security demands, fewer new workers) and expected hikes in interest rates that will make it more expensive to cover the costs of borrowed money.

Nevertheless, many Americans still don't feel they've benefited from the recovery. There is an impression that wages have been stagnant and, post–financial crisis, average consumers have found that they have to jump through more hoops to qualify for loans. An NBC News/*Wall Street Journal* poll taken in July 2016 found that about a third of American adults thought the economy hadn't really improved; 15% said the economy improved but not because of Obama.

Obama's economy seems destined to be the subject of volumes of academic, historical and political research. Were his policies effective? It's tough to measure that in four-year bursts. Just ask students of Franklin D. Roosevelt's New Deal. Was the Obama stimulus enough? Most liberals say it should have been bigger, and conservatives say it was a boondoggle. Although Obama has no direct control over the Federal Reserve, in his second term, he picked Janet Yellen to lead it, suggesting he had an idea about her thinking on interest rates and other matters that would ripple through the economy even after he leaves office. And what of his protections for Main Street, such as the Consumer Financial Protection Bureau and the Dodd-Frank Wall Street reform law? Millions of Americans have benefited from the measures, but Republicans are still critical of them, and small banks and giant financial institutions alike say the programs are burdensome.

In their final days, the president and his team expressed pride in what they had accomplished, even if the American people didn't understand it. "We were moving so fast early on that we couldn't take victory laps," Obama told the *New York Times* as he mulled his economic legacy. "We couldn't explain everything we were doing. I mean, one day we're saving the banks; the next day we're saving the auto industry; the next day we're trying to see whether we can have some impact on the housing market." He clearly did have an impact, even if its full measure can't be known for decades.

THE FIGHT TO INSURE

For all the vicious backlash that it spawned, health-care reform is Obama's signature achievement

By Kate Pickert

It was perhaps the best Christmas present President Barack Obama could have received at the end of his first year in the Oval Office.

On Dec. 24, 2009, after a month of intense procedural gamesmanship, the U.S. Senate approved the Affordable Care Act in a 60–39 vote that fell along party lines. The tally placed Obama an important step closer to his goal of achieving comprehensive health reform that would expand insurance coverage and cut costs.

"These are not small reforms. These are big reforms," Obama said in remarks to reporters shortly after the vote. "This will be the most important piece of social legislation since the Social Security Act passed in the 1930s and the most important reform of our health-care system since Medicare passed in the 1960s."

Then he boarded Air Force One for a holiday break in Hawaii with Michelle, Sasha and Malia.

If Obama is to be remembered for any single piece of legislation, it will be the law that took his name: Obamacare. Though the measure continues to be controversial, the Patient Protection and Affordable Care Act changed the health-care landscape. Twenty million Americans gained coverage as a result of the law, and the rate of uninsured Americans has fallen some 35% since 2014, the year new coverage provisions went into place. The yearly increase in average health-care spending now stands at just 5%, down from an average growth of 7.3% between 2001 and 2009. And even health-care leaders who opposed the law initially say they are thinking differently about their own spending, spurred by the law's incentives and penalties.

"It's of tremendous historic importance in the health-care context," says Drew Altman, the president and CEO of the Kaiser Family Foundation, a health-policy research organization. "Presidents have been trying to break through the political logjam with health-reform legislation forever, and no doubt part of Obama's legacy will be that he pushed through the impasse and passed substantial health reform without bipartisan support."

Of course, achieving health reform came with significant political and practical costs. Debate over the law exposed deep ideological divisions, and the legislation spawned one of the most contentious public-policy fights in history. Opposition to Obama's version of health reform helped spawn the Tea Party movement and was a rallying cry for Republicans running for national office. Hordes of

Under the Affordable Care Act, less than 10% of the U.S. population is without insurance.

MARCH 31 IS THE DEADLINE TO
GET READY FOR
OBAMACARE!

Do you or someone you know need healthcare coverage?

(888) 920-4517

President Obama finishes signing the Affordable Care Act into law on March 23, 2010.

new patients have swamped the offices of primary-care doctors, and many consumers buying new health plans are finding premiums too high and doctor networks too narrow. Though annual increases for premiums in the individual market between 2008 and 2011 tended to run in the single digits, in 2017, premiums for individual market plans sold through a new federal marketplace are expected to increase by an average of 25%. New subsidies will cover the additional costs for many consumers, but not all.

Even some supporters of the law remain dissatisfied with the results. "I think it's fair to say we expected more people to be covered by now," says Len Nichols, a veteran of the Clinton health-reform effort and director of the Center for Health Policy Research and Ethics at George Mason University.

Obama had long made health-care legislation a priority. In 2006, before he declared his candidacy for the presidency, Obama asked for a briefing on a popular comprehensive health-reform plan in Massachusetts he hoped could be replicated nationwide. After beating John McCain in 2008 by 10 million votes, the new president felt he had a mandate for change, and he wanted to start with an ambitious plan to upend and reorganize the U.S. health-care system.

GHOSTS OF HEALTH-REFORM EFFORTS PAST haunted the Obama White House. In 1993, then–First Lady Hillary Clinton had led a push to expand coverage and cut spending, but the effort ended in spectacular failure. Health-insurance lobbyists and Republican members of Congress vehemently opposed Clinton's plan. Some congressional Democrats, meanwhile, resented the White House asking them to adopt Clinton's legislation carte blanche.

Obama thought he had a good workaround. Because the Massachusetts plan was based on a report from a conservative think tank, the Heritage Foundation, he assumed congressional Republicans would cooperate with Democrats. He would ask representatives and senators to work out the details. "They understood the politics through the lens of the '90s failure," says Jonathan Gruber, an economics professor at MIT and a health-care adviser to the Bay State reform effort and later the Obama administration. "They clearly knew, after the Clinton years, they weren't going to lay out a plan."

So the administration itself went to work. Doctors, patients and lawmakers were invited along with health-care lobbyists to the White House in early spring for a public forum on health-care reform. It was the first time that all of the major parties in the health-care debate had been asked to sit in the same room to discuss priorities. A group of Republicans and Democrats on the Senate's powerful finance committee began drafting a plan that would subsidize private health insurance for millions of Americans, expand Medicaid for the poor and reduce the federal deficit through new taxes and cuts to Medicare. Meanwhile, a separate Senate committee and three committees in the House went to work on their own proposals.

But then came the August 2009 congressional recess. Senators and House members returned to their home states to find fierce opposition to reform among their constituents. Health-care-industry lobbyists and political opponents of the president accused Obama of advocating for "a government takeover of health care." Seniors worried that cuts to Medicare would affect their benefits. Business owners resented a congressional proposal that would require them to provide health insurance to employees.

Town-hall discussions on the issue erupted into screaming protests. Former vice-presidential candidate Sarah Palin suggested that seniors would be forced to appear before government "death panels" that would decide whether they were worthy of health care. That same month, Democratic senator Ted Kennedy of Massachusetts, a longtime champion of health reform, died of brain cancer. A Kennedy ally was appointed to take his place temporarily, but a special election for the seat loomed, threatening to erase the Senate supermajority the Democrats had enjoyed all year.

The bipartisan package Obama had hoped for was gone. A plan to enact comprehensive health-care reform would have to move forward without Republican support.

Once it became clear that the future of health reform rested entirely on Democrats in Congress, several of them stepped forward with demands. Pro-life Democrats in the House wanted an amendment to restrict insurance coverage for abortions. In the Senate, several moderate Democratic senators withheld support until they secured special funding.

Finally, though, the Senate made its Christmas Eve approval. About three months later, in March 2010, the legislation squeaked through Congress, and Obama signed it into law.

That set into motion the next battle: implementation. After decisively winning a new House majority in 2010, Republican members opposed to the new law tried to weaken or repeal it. A slim Democratic majority in the Senate stood guard, but public support for health reform remained divided. In 2012, the Supreme Court struck down a mandatory national Medicaid-expansion plan that was central to the law's coverage goals. And in 2013, when Americans were able to purchase new health plans under the law for the first time, a website meant to market and sell plans crashed as soon as it went online.

Then, gradually, the setbacks gave way to grudging acceptance. Today, many of the law's provisions are popular. Young people can stay on their parents' insurance policies until they are 26. Discrimination against those with preexisting conditions has ended. And new federal subsidies to help consumers buy private health insurance have increased affordability.

Though challenges remain, and President-elect Trump has signaled his intention to revisit the law, repealing it might prove even more difficult than passing it. Doing so would entail ending coverage for 20 million Americans; plus, it would increase the federal deficit by $140 billion to $350 billion per year, according to estimates from the Congressional Budget Office, a nonpartisan government agency that analyzes spending. What's more, the charged politics surrounding the law may shift in a post-Obama era.

"How much of the opposition [to] the law will dissipate when it's only about the details of health reform and no longer about Obama?" asks Altman. "Bipartisan support for the law remains utterly broken. [It] may improve over time, but that story has yet to be written."

LEADING THE FREE WORLD

Obama's foreign policy was defined by pragmatism, realpolitik and a lot of wait-and-see

By Haley Sweetland Edwards

When campaigning for the White House in 2008, Barack Obama, then a junior senator from Illinois, all but promised Americans the world.

Under his watch, he said, the United States would end the conflicts in Iraq and Afghanistan, close the prison at Guantánamo Bay, get nations on track to prevent catastrophic climate change, rebuild relations with Muslims around the globe, eliminate nuclear weapons, and create deep and lasting economic and security ties with Asia. When the brand-new president was awarded a Nobel Peace Prize in 2009, the idea that he might soon preside over a peaceful, prosperous global order seemed not only possible but imminent. Hopes were high.

Seven years later, as Obama's second term draws to a close, the reality is more tempered. Instead of transformation, the most resonant characteristic of Obama's relationship to the world has been caution: pragmatism, realpolitik and an extra helping of wait-and-see.

This strategy has cut both ways. Obama's many admirers have roundly applauded his role as an ambassador for American values abroad. After eight years under the often-

Top row, from left: Obama with Cuba's Raúl Castro, 2015, China's Xi Jinping, 2016, and Pope Francis, 2015. Second row, from left: Syrian refugees, 2014; Obama with Queen Elizabeth II, 2011; North Korea's Kim Jong-un, 2015; and Obama with the U.K.'s David Cameron, 2016. Third row, from left: with Russia's Vladimir Putin, 2012, Canada's Justin Trudeau, 2016, and the president of Tanzania, 2013. Fourth row, from left: a soldier in Iraq in 2008; Obama with Mexico's President Enrique Peña Nieto, 2016, and a Saudi prince, 2014

CHINA

10

LIFT-A-LOFT

At the G7 summit in 2015, German chancellor Angela Merkel and Obama share a moment before other world leaders arrive for a photograph.

pugnacious administration of George W. Bush, who led the U.S. military into two protracted, expensive and dubiously successful wars, Obama's cool demeanor on the world stage was exactly what many craved. According to *Atlantic* senior correspondent Jeffrey Goldberg, Obama privately celebrated his natural reticence to act. In the wake of the Bush administration, his primary job as U.S. president was simple, he said: "Don't do stupid s---."

Obama set the tone early in his tenure. In a speech in Cairo in 2009, he reached out to the world's 1.5 billion followers of Islam and pledged "to seek a new beginning between the United States and Muslims." Obama quoted from the Koran, the Talmud and the Bible and promised to heal the wounds that divided the "West" from the "Muslim world." (A spokesman for the Palestinian Authority hailed the address, while a spokesman for the West Bank settlers' council dismissed it.)

Yet Obama's role as diplomat in chief was often more than rhetorical. In another profound break from his predecessor in office, Obama made it his administration's priority to talk directly with foreign leaders representing unsavory regimes—a policy with deep, albeit controversial, historical roots. Franklin Roosevelt, for example, met regularly with Joseph Stalin during World War II, and Richard Nixon's personal relationship with Mao Zedong led in part to the opening of China. Supporters have long argued that, in that same manner, Obama's willingness to allow his top officials to sit down with Iranian president Mahmoud Ahmadinejad paved the way for the nuclear deal with Iran—a move that may prove to be the first step toward stabilizing the Persian Gulf.

Similarly, Obama's willingness to engage with President Raúl Castro's Cuba, thumbing his nose at conservative opponents of his policy of rapprochement, led to a thawing of relations with one of the U.S.'s closest geographic neighbors for the first time since the Cold War. In February 2016, Obama became the first president in a half-century to travel to Cuba, and in September 2016, he nominated the first U.S. ambassador to Cuba.

His diplomatic overtures in Europe and East Asia, particularly under his so-called pivot to Asia, earned Obama respect among U.S. allies, especially in Canada, Europe and Asian-Pacific nations, where he remains extraordinarily popular. According to a June 2016 study by the Pew Research Center, more than 75% of respondents in Germany, France, Spain and the U.K. reported having confidence in the U.S. president to "do the right thing regarding world affairs."

Though it's difficult to quantify the benefits of such generic goodwill, some argue that Obama was able to use that mandate to make strides in advancing issues such as climate change. In September 2016, Obama and Chinese president Xi Jinping met to formally ratify the Paris climate agreement in a move that Alden Meyer, who represents the Union of Concerned Scientists, characterized as a significant victory. The Paris Agreement must be ratified by 55 countries responsible for 55% of global emissions, and the U.S.'s early adoption set a precedent for other big nations like Brazil, Canada and Australia to follow.

But Obama's preference for diplomacy and incremental progress over action has been notably less popular at home, where he has drawn harsh criticism from members of his own political party and his Republican adversaries alike. Many liberal interventionists, including Obama's former top adviser Samantha Power, who now serves as the U.S. ambassador to the United Nations, see Obama's decision not to arm moderate Syrian rebels as bordering on a humanitarian crime.

Neoconservatives, meanwhile, as well as hawkish Democrats see Obama's wishy-washy positioning in places like Libya and Ukraine as dangerous for another reason. They argue that it gave the leaders of other countries the impression that the U.S., under the 44th president, would not act quickly, decisively and with extraordinary military force if necessary. Roger Cohen, an op-ed columnist on international affairs for the *New York Times* who has been sharply critical of what he calls Obama's "doctrine of restraint," suggested that Obama's inaction in the Middle East early in his administration is one reason Russian president Vladimir Putin felt he could get away with invading Ukraine. "Not since the end of the Cold War a quarter-century ago has Russia been as assertive or Washington as acquiescent," Cohen wrote. Obama's defenders pointed out that Bush's doctrine of preemptive attack did not deter Russia's invasion of another small neighbor, Georgia, in 2008.

Republican critics have also been quick to condemn Obama's foreign-policy philosophy as "leading from behind," citing as evidence of his unwillingness to take a leading role his premature departure from Iraq and his failure to help piece Libya back together after the 2011 NATO-led conflict in which Muammar el-Qaddafi was overthrown. According to Theodore R. Bromund, a senior research fellow at the conservative Heritage Foundation, the problem was that Obama's strategy was to "retrench" international problems in order to focus more squarely on the U.S., which was, for most of his presidency, struggling to claw its way out of a recession.

As Obama winds down his tenure as commander in chief, at question is how his administration will be judged by history. There is no doubt that Obama ascended to power during an extraordinarily complicated time, when the state of the world's affairs often left him no good choice—just the lesser of two evils. In an interview with *The Atlantic* in the spring of 2016, Obama defended his own choices in that light. The idea that the U.S. could have engaged more forcefully in the Middle East or rattled American sabers more loudly to keep Russia and China in line requires a flawed logic, he said. "The notion that we could have—in a clean way that didn't commit U.S. military forces—changed the equation on the ground there was never true," Obama said, in reference to Syria.

By many of his own—albeit perhaps unrealistically grand—standards, Obama has failed to deliver on many promises. The U.S. remains embroiled in Afghanistan. The detention center at Guantánamo Bay remains open. The Islamic State, a terrorist organization that was hardly known in 2008, has risen as a deadly force. But Obama also leaves the world much improved, and his successes will be felt for generations. He advanced the ball on climate change, kept the U.S. military out of protracted wars and remade the image of America abroad.

THE COMMANDER IN CHIEF

Did Obama help curb terrorism—or set the stage for a more dangerous world?

By Mark Thompson

At the end of the Iraq War, in December 2011, U.S. soldiers board a C-310 heading from Baghdad to Kuwait.

In 2008, exhausted by the long wars and the loss of American soldiers in Afghanistan and Iraq, U.S. citizens voted Barack Obama into office over the hawkish John McCain. They liked the idea of a different kind of commander in chief, one who not only seemed leery of sending GIs abroad but also vowed to end the two divisive conflicts he'd inherited.

Obama prevailed militarily, at least at the outset, and over the course of his eight years dramatically cut U.S. troops in Afghanistan and Iraq, from 180,000 to about 15,000. But he achieved that in fitful waves. In Iraq, Obama followed through on President George W. Bush's plan, negotiated with Baghdad, to essentially pull out by 2012. But he was forced to begin sending troops back, starting in mid-2014, as the Islamic State swept in from Syria and occupied the northern part of the country.

Obama embraced Afghanistan as "the good war." He doubled the number of U.S. troops there, to more than 100,000 in 2011, which succeeded in keeping the Taliban at bay; he then brought 90% of them home. But the deployments came at the cost of the lives of more than 1,000 U.S. troops.

Today, both Iraq and Afghanistan are arguably worse off than eight years ago. Afghanistan, where the remaining 8,400 U.S. troops constitute most of the foreign military presence, is impoverished and in the grip of the opium trade. The Taliban is a potent force, controlling or heavily influencing about half of the nation. In Iraq, the central government is weakened. The wide swath of desert between Iraq and Syria has become an incubator for ISIS, posing a greater threat than Iraqi despot Saddam Hussein ever did.

These, of course, were results that some analysts warned of before the initial invasions of Iraq and Afghanistan—both ordered by George W. Bush. The Afghan war, launched in 2001, was supposed to avenge the 9/11 terrorist attacks by Osama bin Laden's Afghanistan-based Al Qaeda. Instead, the effort faltered as Bush diverted U.S. firepower to Iraq to depose Hussein, unleashing the widespread civil unrest that continues to roil the country.

That was Bush's parting gift to the incoming commander in chief, and it proved a difficult bequest for Obama to handle. Many questions remain about the efficacy of his strategy: During Obama's two terms, did he lay the foundation to curb terrorism or contribute to making the world less safe? What more, or else, could he have done? How much of what he leaves behind is the spoiled fruit of an approach guided by wishful thinking?

"I spend a lot of time brooding over these issues," Obama told reporters at his final NATO summit, in July 2016. America's enemies today, he argued, are "not an existential threat but can do real harm and real damage to our societies and create the kind of fear that can cause division."

President Obama greets American troops during a surprise visit to Bagram Air Base, north of Kabul, Afghanistan, in 2010.

IF BUSH LEANED TOWARD A SCORCHED-earth approach when it came to military conflicts, Obama's policy might be best characterized as a controlled burn. From the early days of his administration, Obama vowed to pare back America's post-9/11 "perpetual wartime footing" to a more measured, yet indefinite, campaign to destroy organizations such as Al Qaeda and the Taliban. He took the long view—that the fight against Islamic extremism would be more marathon than sprint—and maintained that a steady, persistent campaign would eventually take down such terrorist groups. "This war, like all wars, must end," he said of what he refrained from calling the War on Terror.

For Obama, the way to combat shadowy foes was not with World War II–style clashes of army divisions and widespread bombings. This new breed of enemy, unlikely to hew to conventional tactics, required different strategies. Obama tried to develop ways to fight what he called "hybrid" conflicts. He deployed U.S. Special Forces. He dramatically boosted the use of unmanned drones, controlled by desk pilots in Nevada and other bases in the U.S.

Under Obama, the Pentagon and CIA targeted individual foxholes, with eyedropper precision, in more than 40,000 strikes, primarily in Iraq and Syria but also in Afghanistan, Libya, Pakistan, Somalia and Yemen. The Pentagon issued daily statements detailing what and who had been demolished in the previous 24 hours.

In some ways they were an expensive eight years, with Obama's defense spending totaling $5.3 trillion—4% more than what Bush spent. But it is difficult to come up with a smart cost-benefit analysis. Many experts blame Bush's actions for helping to create the Islamic State, meaning some of Obama's military investment was devoted to cleaning up his predecessor's mess. The Pentagon says it has killed 45,000 ISIS fighters, but that may be a wrong way to measure impact, given that these are not traditional enemy armies. Only 19 hijackers, after all, were needed to carry out Al Qaeda's 9/11 attacks.

In Iraq, from where Obama was eager to bring U.S. troops home and declare victory, 270 soldiers died under his command, 6% of the approximately 4,500 U.S. troops killed there since the conflict began in 2003. Obama was likewise adamant against deploying any more than a handful of U.S. troops into Syria, even as Syria's president, Bashar al-Assad, unleashed chemical weapons on his own citizens. As the war on ISIS grew more intense, Obama reluctantly approved sending U.S. troops back into the region; there are now more than 5,000 of them advising local fighters inside Iraq and Syria.

Obama tried a different approach in Afghanistan, which he embraced as a just conflict because of the shelter that that country's Taliban leadership gave the 9/11 plotters. Fearing that the Taliban could retake the country, Obama boosted the number of American troops in Afghanistan from 70,000 to 100,000. By the time they all departed three years later, more than 1,600 American soldiers had died, roughly three quarters of the total who were killed in action. That surge did stay the Taliban, but it did not, in the end, deter them. "You have the watches," a captured Taliban fighter famously said. "We have the time."

THEN THERE WAS THE SECRET ATTACK-drone program, designed to kill without leaving American fingerprints (and without the formal approval of either the U.S. public or its representatives in Congress). While the administration estimated in July that ill-aimed drones had killed as many as 116 civilians in Libya, Somalia, Pakistan and Yemen between 2009 and 2015, independent analysts suggested the toll was three times as high. This "collateral damage," critics warned, would inspire even more people to align with terrorists.

"YOU HAVE THE WATCHES," A TALIBAN FIGHTER SAID. "WE HAVE THE TIME."

Beyond his approach to fighting ISIS, Obama's martial reticence has been blamed for bolstering aggression around the world. Many in Congress and elsewhere criticized the president for not doing more to curb the Syrian civil war, which has led to 470,000 Syrians' deaths and has also created millions of refugees. The Russians and Chinese expanded their spheres of influence without significant U.S. pushback. North Korea kept firing test missiles, and Iran—despite the 2015 nuclear accord forged by Obama—showed little sign of reforming its theocratic ways. Libya turned violent and has been largely ungoverned since the U.S. and NATO helped Libyan rebels remove longtime dictator Muammar el-Qaddafi in 2011.

Sometimes it seemed that Obama simply discounted the advice of top military aides. His minimal, calendar-driven deployments frustrated many officers, who felt they were seeing a decade of sacrifice erode. "I never doubted Obama's support for the troops," Robert Gates, a Bush holdover who served as Obama's first civilian defense chief, wrote cuttingly in his memoir, "only his support for their mission."

Obama's military disconnect surfaced in smaller episodes, too. The White House's decision to hail Army sergeant Bowe Bergdahl, for whose release the U.S. traded five Taliban leaders in 2014, upset many in uniform. Many troops and vets viewed Bergdahl—who had spent five years in Taliban captivity—as a traitor and were stunned by the White House's ceremony announcing his return. Following an Army investigation, Bergdahl is slated to face a court-martial for desertion in 2017.

ALL PRESIDENTS, OF COURSE, ARE BOUND to have some disagreements with Pentagon brass. Obama cannot be blamed for sparking tensions with longtime adversaries like North Korea and Russia. What's more, he did not operate in a vacuum. With the pains of the Bush wars still fresh, Congress preferred not to get its hands dirty by authorizing combat, so it subcontracted the task to Obama. He was forced to rely on a congressional authorization passed shortly after 9/11 in order to carry out attacks. The uniformed military services also sought to keep troops from harm's way and increased their reliance on private, for-profit contractors to handle critical support missions.

As his term wound down, Obama continued to defend his record. In a National Security Council session at the Pentagon in August 2016, he warned that even as the U.S. weakens ISIS in Syria and Iraq, going forward the group is likely to place "an even greater emphasis on encouraging high-profile terrorist attacks, including in the United States." "This cannot be solved by military force alone," Obama said, but rather needs to include social, political and economic reforms.

Those are long-range goals. So it's not surprising that Obama leaves the White House, like Bush before him, with an incomplete grade in the War on Terror. If it turns out that the nation's 44th president has successfully smothered violent Islamic zealotry, his national-security record will be sterling. If not, historians will forever second-guess what more he should have done.

This photo leads to an augmented-reality experience through the Time Inc. Special Edition App.

See the Contents page for details. Then point the camera of your phone or tablet to capture the photo at right.

HOW IT WENT DOWN

TIME pieced together the countdown of the May 2, 2011, killing of Osama bin Laden

By Graham Allison

Top White House and national-security advisers join the president and vice president in the Situation Room for live updates on the raid.

I can only speak with authority through Feb. 15, 2009," said Michael Hayden, George W. Bush's last CIA director. "But at that point, when people would ask, 'When's the last time you really knew where he was?' my answer was Tora Bora in 2001."

Obama's first order to his new CIA director, Leon Panetta, in 2009 was to "make the killing or capture of OBL the top priority of the war against Al Qaeda." That order grew out of an Obama campaign pledge that "if we have Osama bin Laden in our sights and the Pakistani government is unable or unwilling to take him out, then we have to act, and we will take him out. We will kill bin Laden; we will crush Al Qaeda. That has to be our biggest national-security priority."

There have been many histories of the events that led to bin Laden's death on May 2, 2011, but the purpose of this analysis is to examine White House decision-making for lessons that can be applied to future foreign-policy challenges.

Three factors led to the mission's success.

1. New intelligence and military capabilities developed during the decade after 9/11 gave

Obama choices and weapons that were not available to his predecessors in the White House.

2. Following missteps in Afghanistan, Obama put in place a disciplined national-security decision-making process that was analytically rigorous, insistent on written product and flexible.

3. The commander in chief had the confidence and determination to slow the clock long enough to aim carefully before pulling the trigger.

Hard Choices

Fifteen months after Obama's initial "Get bin Laden" order, Panetta returned to the White House in August 2010 with good news. The CIA had discovered a multihouse compound in northeast Pakistan in which bin Laden's favorite courier was living. The area, surrounded by an 18-foot wall and dubbed the Fortress by Obama's counterterrorism czar John Brennan, was in Abbottabad, a city about as far from Pakistan's capital as Baltimore is from Washington.

Obama now faced three major decisions:

1. When to act? Every day of delay increased the likelihood that bin Laden, if he was actually there, would escape. A leak in Washington that popped up on a blog or in the press would cause him to flee.

2. Whom to include in the decision-making? Adding more people would reduce the chances that important dimensions of the operation would go unexamined. But every additional pair of eyes came with a mouth that could be the source of a leak.

3. How, exactly, to capture or kill bin Laden? Obama's menu had four entrées: Predator drones with Hellfire missiles delivering 500-pound bombs, B-2 bombers with 2,000-pound laser-guided bombs, special forces on the ground and a joint military operation with Pakistan.

Though this was first and foremost a matter of national security, any decision would have political consequences. If Obama waited and bin Laden escaped, Obama would be savaged for fiddling while public enemy No. 1 vanished. If he acted and the operation failed, opponents would tar him as a second Jimmy Carter, recalling the failed 1980 attempt to rescue Americans held hostage in Iran.

The biggest surprise of the entire operation was that it was a surprise. A half-century ago, when the CIA discovered that the Soviet Union was sneaking nuclear-tipped missiles into Cuba at the start of what became the Cuban missile crisis, one of the first questions President John F. Kennedy asked was, "How long until this leaks?" His national-security adviser thought a week at most. So JFK gave himself five days to deliberate, review the evidence, listen to counterarguments and change his mind more than once.

In today's Washington, a week is a lifetime. Secrets are often published overnight, as Obama learned painfully in 2009 when circumstances forced him into a decision he opposed: After asking his new commander in Afghanistan, General Stanley McChrystal, to assess the situation in that country, Obama received a dire 66-page brief that urged a major initiative as a way to avoid imminent defeat. The warning shocked the president, but before Obama could meet with his national-security team, McChrystal's report appeared in the press. From that point on, the president had only two choices: to back his new commander or back down.

That outcome, in part, eventually led Obama to replace James Jones, his national-security adviser, with Jones's deputy, Tom Donilon. Obama then asked Donilon to revise the national-security decision-making process to ensure that he could think before acting, could analyze every angle of an issue and probe the competing views of his advisers but in the end make his own call.

"It's Time to Call in the Pros"

In the weeks that followed Panetta's visit to the White House with the news of bin Laden's whereabouts, CIA Deputy Director Michael Morell gave regular intelligence updates to Donilon and Brennan but virtually no one else. The Abbottabad material was so compartmented that it was excluded from the threat matrix in the president's super-secret daily brief out of fear that it would raise flags at the departments of State and Defense and other agencies.

THE FINAL MOMENTS

The last steps took only an hour. How the SEAL team got it done

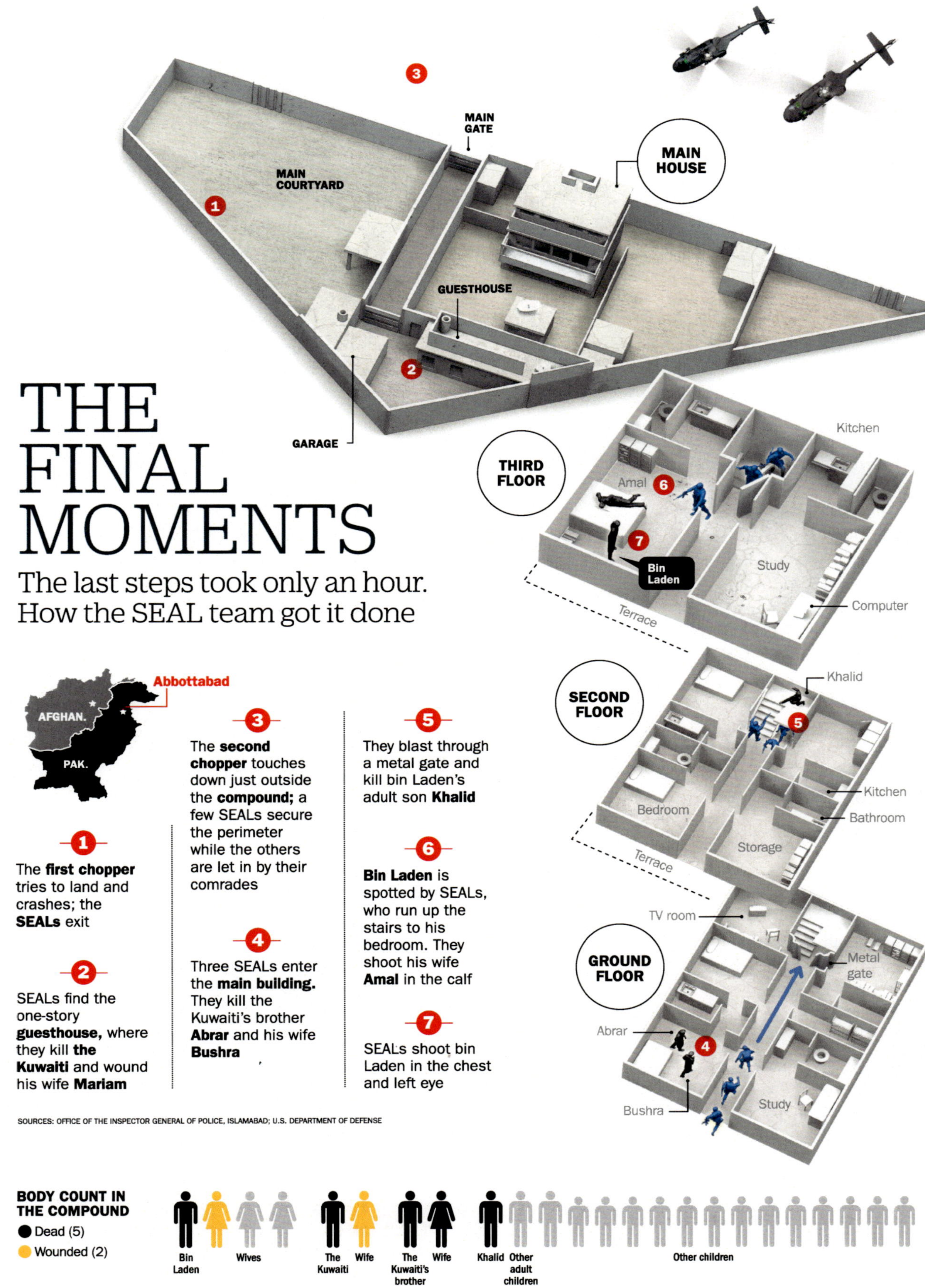

1 The **first chopper** tries to land and crashes; the **SEALs** exit

2 SEALs find the one-story **guesthouse,** where they kill **the Kuwaiti** and wound his wife **Mariam**

3 The **second chopper** touches down just outside the **compound;** a few SEALs secure the perimeter while the others are let in by their comrades

4 Three SEALs enter the **main building.** They kill the Kuwaiti's brother **Abrar** and his wife **Bushra**

5 They blast through a metal gate and kill bin Laden's adult son **Khalid**

6 **Bin Laden** is spotted by SEALs, who run up the stairs to his bedroom. They shoot his wife **Amal** in the calf

7 SEALs shoot bin Laden in the chest and left eye

SOURCES: OFFICE OF THE INSPECTOR GENERAL OF POLICE, ISLAMABAD; U.S. DEPARTMENT OF DEFENSE

BODY COUNT IN THE COMPOUND

● Dead (5)
● Wounded (2)

Bin Laden · Wives · The Kuwaiti · Wife · The Kuwaiti's brother · Wife · Khalid · Other adult children · Other children

By December 2010, Morell's team at the CIA's counterterrorism center was 60% confident that bin Laden was living in the compound. Obama instructed the CIA to make certain but to be careful not to flush the prey.

In a series of 40 intelligence reviews from August 2010 to April 2011, further questions were explored and competing hypotheses examined—in particular, the possibility that the suspect in Abbottabad was not bin Laden. This led to the creation of what some called the Bible: a three-inch binder listing every question about the operation, from assessing the risks of a leak at various stages to what to do with bin Laden's body.

CHALLENGES INCLUDED HANDLING LEAKS AND WHAT TO DO WITH THE BODY.

On specific instructions from the president, only six people at the White House were in the loop from August to December: Obama, Donilon, Brennan, deputy national-security adviser Denis McDonough, Vice President Joe Biden and Biden's national-security adviser Tony Blinken, supported by Panetta and Morell. Up until then, Panetta and Morell had assumed that the CIA's small and rarely discussed cadre of paramilitary personnel would conduct the raid. But as they studied their options that winter after hearing the agency's plan to raid the compound, Morell turned to Panetta and said, "It's time to call in the pros."

The circle was expanded to include two additional players—Admiral William McRaven, who led the Joint Special Operations Command, and Joint Chiefs of Staff Vice Chairman James Cartwright, who was an Obama favorite—but not Cartwright's boss, JCS chairman Mike Mullen, Secretary of State Hillary Clinton or even Secretary of Defense Robert Gates. In order to divert the money needed for the operation—and ensure its legality—Panetta gave the leaders of the congressional intelligence committees a general idea about the mission.

Sending in the SEALs

In the president's mind, the four options for killing bin Laden quickly shrank to three and then to two. On Jan. 27, 2011, CIA contractor Raymond Davis was arrested in Lahore on murder charges, an incident that reminded the White House that its Pakistani allies could never be reliable partners in such a highly sensitive mission. A joint operation with Lahore was crossed off the list.

Several weeks later, Obama shelved the Predator plan, which called for Hellfire missile strikes on the mysterious figure whose daily walks around the compound's courtyard led the CIA to name him the Pacer. Among other reasons, Obama doubted that 500-pound bombs could guarantee a kill. What's more, since Pakistan was unlikely to cooperate in sifting through the remains, how would the U.S. know if it had killed the right man? Similar arguments led the president to tilt against a B-2 strike.

Thus, step by step, Obama arrived at the choice that promised the highest reward but also carried the highest risks: sending in the SEALs. On March 29, Obama directed McRaven to perform a "full dress rehearsal."

A war cabinet of National Security Council members held five meetings over the final six weeks to review all the options once more. Participants report that in these sessions Obama invited competing views and reexaminations of his previous conclusions. Even in this phase, the loop was tight: Gates and Clinton had to attend the meetings alone, without their deputies or staff. As more officials needed to be briefed on the operation, every new name required Donilon's personal approval.

On April 28, in a final meeting in the Situation Room, Obama asked each adviser what they would do and took an up-or-down vote on whether to launch the raid. After concluding the mission was a go—over Gates's and Biden's "no" votes—he widened the circle to include Attorney General Eric Holder, Secretary of Homeland Security Janet Napolitano, FBI director Robert Mueller and others, and on May 2, the kill mission was accomplished.

It was only after U.S. helicopters escaped Pakistani airspace that officials began dialing key individuals to inform them before making a public announcement. Obama's first calls

From top: Pakistani students stand outside the compound days after the raid; members of the military tune in to the president's announcement from Kandahar Airfield; a crowd watches the same broadcast from the White House's South Lawn.

were to former presidents George W. Bush and Bill Clinton. Mullen called Pakistan's army chief of staff, General Ashfaq Kayani, who seemed stunned. Five minutes after members of Congress were contacted and an hour before the president's formal announcement, CNN broke the news.

Lessons

First, this case demonstrates that the U.S. government is capable of extraordinary performance in extraordinary times. The challenge is finding ways to improve performance in ordinary cases.

Second, sometimes secrets matter. And when they do, secrecy matters more. The bin Laden case demonstrates why success requires both discovering secrets and then keeping them, allowing a president time to reflect in private and permitting him to reach a decision and act.

Third, secrecy comes with a price. Tightening the decision loop in order to prevent leaks means that important angles may not be adequately considered. If Joint Chiefs of Staff personnel had been brought in earlier and told to design an alternative storyline about Pakistani cooperation, the U.S. might have avoided humiliating the Pakistani military in its own backyard. Going forward, whatever American officials say or do, Pakistanis will presume the worst about the U.S.'s intentions.

Fourth, the most troubling lesson from this case is the dog that hasn't barked. In the aftermath of Abbottabad, we are left with two possibilities: either the Pakistanis knew that bin Laden was there or they didn't. If Pakistan's military and intelligence leadership was complicit in harboring bin Laden, we have learned a great deal about where we stand with our nominal ally.

But after intense review of the materials seized in the raid, the brute fact is that not a shred of evidence has been found to suggest that anyone in the Pakistani military and intelligence hierarchy knew of bin Laden's whereabouts. Thus we are forced to consider the perhaps even more troubling possibility that Pakistan's military and intelligence leadership did not know that the U.S.'s most wanted man was living in their country.

CHAPTER TWO

HISTORY IN THE MAKING

“Here in America, our success should depend not on accident of birth but the strength of our work ethic and the scope of our dreams. That’s what drew our forebears here.”

—Barack Obama, 2014 State of the Union address

HAS CHANGE COME TO AMERICA?

The president's record on race was imperfect, but the symbolism of his terms in office was potent

By Maya Rhodan

On the 50th anniversary of "Bloody Sunday," in 2015, the president, Rep. John Lewis (at his right) and the first family honor freedom marchers in Selma, Ala.

Addressing a crowd in South Carolina during the 2007 presidential primary season, Michelle Obama summoned cheers by presenting an inspiring and historic vision: four African Americans, the Obamas, living in the White House. "Imagine our family on that inaugural platform," she urged. "America will look at itself differently."

And for a moment, it did. "Change has come," president-elect Barack Obama declared in his 2008 victory speech, invoking the 1964 civil rights anthem by Sam Cooke. For many, Obama's election signaled the start of a post-racial era in the United States. The African-American community was filled with pride. Whites were optimistic. In a Gallup survey, 67% of Americans said they believed race relations between blacks and whites "would eventually be worked out," the highest percentage ever registered by the polling and research company. But there were also hints that the hope went only so far. Though 95% of African Americans who voted in the presidential election cast their ballots for Obama, only 43% of white voters did—as opposed to 55% who backed Obama's opponent, Sen. John McCain. And in Gallup's 2008 "hopeful" survey, 60% of all voters who picked McCain were pessimistic about the future under Obama. More than half—56%—were "afraid."

America's first black president was at the center of the "thorny subject of race," as President Bill Clinton had once called it, and Obama was in a delicate spot. He was at once expected to moderate the ongoing national debate on race while also being a vested expert on the issue. There was an inherent impracticality to those dual roles, and it quickly became clear that a black president alone could not and would not undo decades of tension.

Skinny Kid with a Funny Name

Obama introduced himself to America as a "skinny kid with a funny name" in 2004, as the keynote speaker at the Democratic National Convention in Boston. His was a story that seemed to epitomize the progressive possibilities of the United States: a Kenyan man marries a white woman from middle America, and they produce a son who rises through the ranks of the political system to become one of Illinois's two U.S. senators. The theme of unification triumphing over entrenched division became a through-line of Obama's approach to race relations. Yet instead of bringing an end to American tribalism, Obama's election in 2008 seemed to prompt partisan animosity that was often racially tinged. A baseless conspiracy theory held that Obama secretly practiced Islam and was not a natural-born U.S. citizen. (He's Protestant and was born in Hawaii.) When Obama reacted to the arrest of black Harvard professor Henry Louis Gates Jr. in 2009—the president said the Cambridge, Mass., police officer "acted stupidly"—ultraconservative radio host Glenn Beck suggested Obama had a "deep-seated hatred for white people or the white culture." Some Republicans' reactions to Obama's presidency were persistent and visceral, and Ta-Nehisi Coates, known for his thoughtful writings on race, examined the phenomenon in *The Atlantic*. Among other things, Coates noted that Rep. Steve King of Iowa claimed that the president "favors the black person" and that radio host Rush Limbaugh, also a far-right conservative, declared without substantiation that Obama had launched an era of reverse racism, in which white kids "now get beat up, with the black kids cheering 'yeah, right on, right on, right on.' "

Black America in the Age of Obama

While conservative critics alleged that the president was given to playing the race card, prominent members of the African-American community wondered if such a card was even in his deck. Yes, he marked significant moments in civil rights history and pointedly celebrated Black History Month. But Obama's approach to issues that mattered most to African Americans—such as high unemployment and lagging educational outcomes—rarely strayed from middle-of-the-road pragmatism. He seemed to avoid appearing too concerned about blacks. "Whenever I gave an interview, I felt the pressure to say 'all Americans, all Americans,' " Van Jones, an Obama administration official in 2009, later told *New York* magazine. "I understood the tightrope from the beginning. He's the president of all people. But sometimes it felt like he was president of everyone except black people."

Clockwise from top left: the "beer summit" to discuss the arrest of professor Henry Louis Gates; the funeral of Rev. Clementa Pinckney; a rally in memory of Trayvon Martin

White House senior adviser Valerie Jarrett disputed that characterization and said the president worked to represent all citizens. "He fully appreciates what it's like to try to flag a cab on the South Side of Chicago when you're a black man. It's not easy," she said. "But he's also the president of the United States of America."

After Obama secured his second term, many members of the black community began to comment that the president was loosening up, finally able to address issues facing communities of color more comfortably and without alienating his white supporters. One turning point seemed to be the 2013 acquittal of George Zimmerman, the Florida man who shot unarmed black teen Trayvon Martin. The killing struck a chord with Obama, who told the nation that if his own life had played out differently, he could have faced a similar fate. "Trayvon Martin could have been me 35 years ago," the president said in a moving ad-

This photo leads to an augmented-reality experience through the Time Inc. Special Edition App.

See the Contents page for details. Then point the camera of your phone or tablet to capture the photo at left.

dress in which he called on all Americans to do some "soul-searching."

Martin's death spurred Obama to look for solutions to level the playing field for black and brown boys, which, among other initiatives, resulted in My Brother's Keeper, a White House–sponsored mentorship program. Yet even as the president began to address race more openly, current events underscored the difficulties facing the black community's most prominent figure. In 2014, when a grand jury in Ferguson, Mo., declined to indict white officer Darren Wilson in the death of African-American 18-year-old Michael Brown, protests erupted in the streets of Missouri and across the U.S. On television, split-screen images were startling. On one side, viewers could see officers in riot gear and rows of buildings being set ablaze; on the other, a staid President Obama issuing a call for calm.

Two years later, another spate of shootings of black men by law enforcement seemed to widen the rift between the president and black activists. First there was a killing in Baton Rouge, then one in Minneapolis. And those incidents were followed by a sniper's fatal attack on Dallas police during a protest against police brutality. Many in the Black Lives Matter movement believed that, though the killings happened under Obama, they could not necessarily look to him for answers. Obama and the government he represented, it seemed to some, were part of the problem.

Symbols Matter

And yet there remains no question that the Obama era represented a profound shift in U.S. race relations—a point Michelle Obama drove home during the 2016 Democratic National Convention. Her husband's achievement, she said, was the story of generations of people who felt the lash of bondage but who kept on striving "so that today I wake up every morning in a house that was built by slaves, and I watch my daughters, two beautiful, intelligent, black young women, playing with their dogs on the White House lawn."

Obama's record on race relations was imperfect, but the symbolism of his presidency is potent. That's apparent in the image of a young black boy, wearing his Sunday best in the Oval Office, touching the head of a bowing Barack Obama to gauge the similarity of their hair textures—a photo that hung for years in the West Wing. And it's also evident every time one sees the bright eyes of an African-American boy or girl gazing up at the president from behind a rope line as his hand grazes a chubby cheek. For a generation of Americans, the president's race mattered in the most meaningful way.

THE PRESIDENT AND THE DANCER

President Obama and ballerina Misty Copeland sat with TIME reporter Maya Rhodan on Feb. 29, 2016, to talk about race, gender and success in the White House Cabinet Room. Here are the highlights of the conversation

TIME: Thank you both so much for joining us today. My hope is that this is more of a conversation than an interview. So we'll just let you guys talk. And I want to start off by saying that you have a lot more in common than a lot of people know. You were both born into multiracial families, you were raised by single mothers, and you've risen to the top of your respective fields as African Americans. But I'm curious: What do you see in each other that you recognize in yourself? What is it, and is there a common thread that has allowed you both to succeed?
PRESIDENT OBAMA: Well, first of all, I thought you were going to say that I'm also a really good dancer. *[Laughter.]*

TIME: I thought about it. I saw you dancing with a 106-year-old. *[Laughter.]*
OBAMA: You know, as the father of two daughters, one of the things I'm always looking for are strong women who are out there who are breaking barriers and doing great stuff. And Misty's a great example of that. Somebody who has entered a field that's very competitive, where the assumptions are that she may not belong. And through sheer force of will and determination and incredible talent and hard work, she was able to arrive at the pinnacle of her field. And that's exciting. The other thing is, as a father of two daughters, seeing how images of strong, athletic, accomplished women carry over, and encouraging them in sports and dance and how they move physically—it turns out that every study shows that young girls who are involved in sports, dance, athletics end up having more confidence generally.
MISTY COPELAND: I think that there is a sense of humbleness and humility, and there's a human that's within you. And I think that that's something that I can relate to and connect with that people are drawn to. And again, just being grounded. And I feel like as I'm embarking on my first season as a principal dancer, I'm experiencing something that I didn't prepare myself for, I think, emotionally and mentally and psychologically. When you have all of these expectations and goals to reach this point that 1% get to, you know, how do you—what do you do when you get there?
OBAMA: Well, you know, it's interesting, this whole notion of when you arrive. I don't know how it felt for you, but certainly for me, you know, I burst out onto the national scene with the Democratic Convention speech of 2004. And that was the first time that I had a big national audience. And everybody responded really favorably. And so I got a lot of attention and interviews and magazine pieces and all this stuff. I still remember telling Michelle and my closest friends, I said, "I'm not any smarter today than I was last week." In some

ways, when you struggle for a while, and you've had the ability of being an ordinary person, and you've gone shopping, changed diapers and tried to figure out how to pay the bills and so forth, you're not some overnight success.

TIME: And you both represent the African-American community. As the president of the United States, as a principal dancer for the American Ballet Theatre, do you ever think that—how does race come into play? Do you think that people still treat you differently because of race?

COPELAND: A lot of what I've experienced has not always been to my face, or it's been very subtle. But it's in a way that I know what's going on, and I feel it deep inside of me. And being the only African American in almost every environment in terms of classical ballet—it weighs on you, and it wears on you after a while.

OBAMA: Well, part of classical ballet that makes it challenging is that there's a very set way of doing things. There's sort of this canon that people want it just a certain way, or they want it to look a certain way. So do you find now that you're in a position where you can start pushing the barriers a little bit and the boundaries in terms of what people expect?

COPELAND: Absolutely. I mean, I think that having a platform and having a voice to be seen by people beyond the classical-ballet world has really been my power.... I think it's given me more of a voice. And it's, I think, forcing a lot of these top-tier companies to address the lack of diversity and diversify the bodies that we're seeing in classical ballet. It's really forcing that conversation to be had.

"Being African-American has definitely been a huge obstacle for me," says Copeland.

TIME: Looking back, was there anything that someone told either of you about race, or didn't tell you about race that you wish they had, or that you feel like you had to learn on your own?

COPELAND: I feel like my mom pretty much covered everything with me. Being biracial, she made it very clear to me that, yes, you're Italian and you're German and you are black, but you are going to be viewed by the world and by society as a black woman, and you should be prepared for that.

OBAMA: You know, I mean, I think about this now as a parent... and for me, what I always try to transmit to my kids is that issues of race, discrimination, the tragic history of slavery and Jim Crow, all those things are real.... And recognize that they didn't stop overnight. Certainly not just when I was elected. I remember people talking about how somehow this was going to solve all our racial problems. I wasn't one of those who subscribed to that notion.... You have to understand that, and you have to recognize that each of us has some good and some bad in us. And that's not an excuse, but what it does do is, it gives us an opportunity then to have a conversation and to reach across the divide.

TIME: And wrapping things up, what do you see as the single greatest fixable obstacle to the success of young people today?

COPELAND: The single—wow. I think—everything that you were saying, being able to have an understanding of yourself and how you fit into society and who you are. But to be empathetic to everyone around you, I think, is such a powerful thing to hold.

OBAMA: Well, you know, I spend most of my time thinking about institutions. And there's no doubt, even though it's a cliché, that the single biggest difference we can make is making sure that our kids get a good education.... We can do a lot more to open up people's perspective about who belongs where. And press to make sure that we have more women CEOs and more African-American film directors and more Latino police officers. But the foundation that all this depends on is making sure that on the front end, when these little babies are born and start to get curious about the world and are like sponges, that we are giving them the kind of education and the nurturing that they need.

Adapted from Time.com

TRUE COLORS

Across the nation and in the White House, attitudes toward LGBT rights and issues rapidly became more inclusive

By Philip Elliott

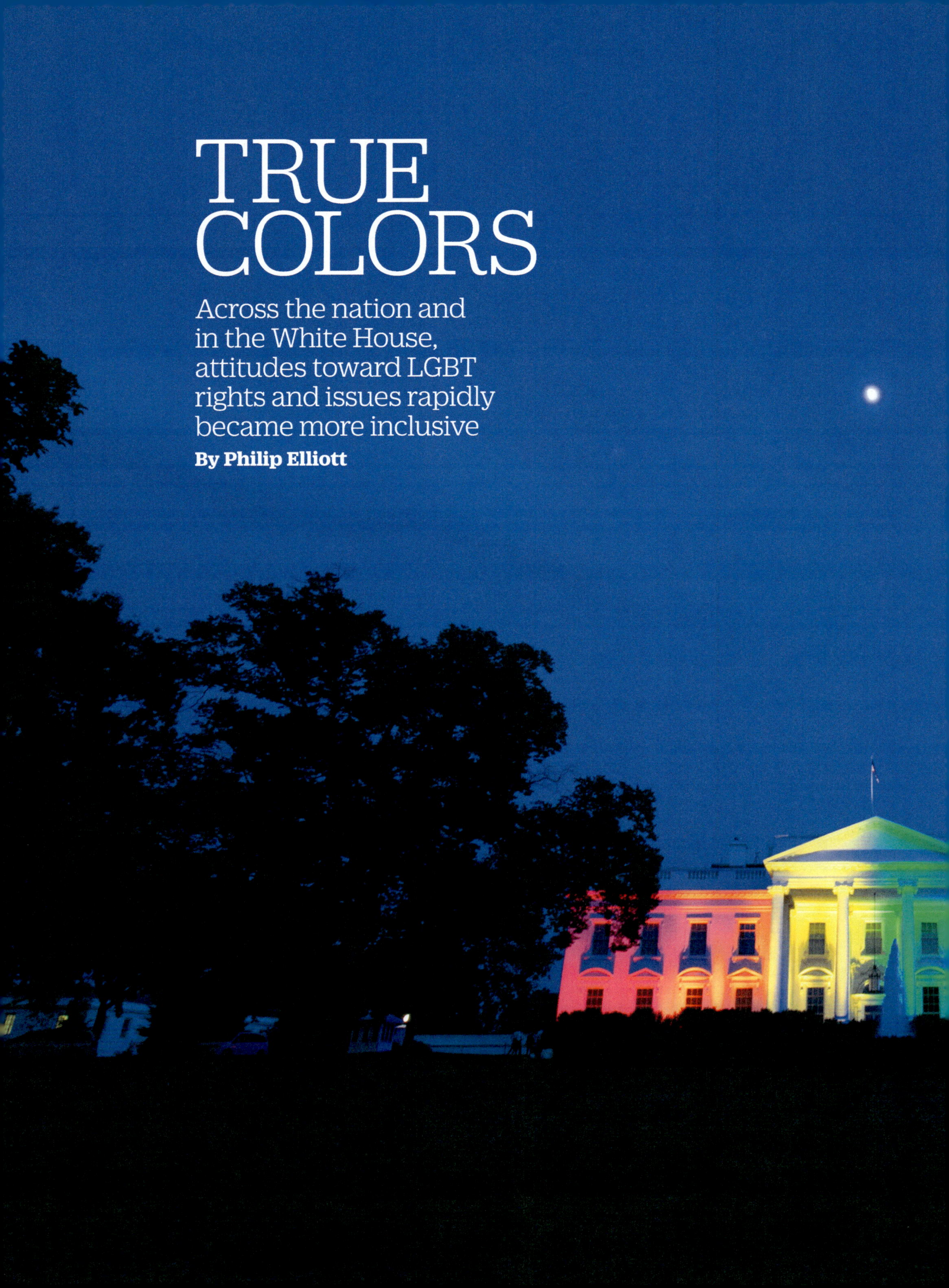

On the way back from a television taping in the spring of 2012, Joe Biden turned to an aide. The team had better alert the White House: in two days, NBC's *Meet the Press* would air an interview during which the vice president endorsed gay marriage. "Who do you love? Who do you love, and will you be loyal to the person you love?" the nation would soon hear Biden telling host David Gregory. "That's what people are finding out what all marriages at their root are about."

In the West Wing, Barack Obama's loyalists fumed and fretted. The president, long officially opposed to same-sex marriage, had been weighing how and when to shift his public position. It was supposed to be Obama, not Biden, who got headlines for ushering in a new era of acceptance of the gay community. Now Biden's off-the-cuff comment would force Obama's hand, and at just the wrong moment—just months before a 2012 re-election bid.

"What is Joe thinking?" one senior Obama aide asked another. Scrambling to recoup, aides phoned ABC News's Robin Roberts to arrange an interview in which Obama would follow Biden, becoming the first sitting U.S. president to say that same-sex couples should have the right to marry. The news was so momentous that ABC broke into scheduled programming and scored wall-to-wall coverage of the scoop.

"I've been going through an evolution on this issue. I've always been adamant that

The White House, proudly illuminated after the same-sex-marriage ruling in 2015

Gay-pride-parade participants hold signs in support of presidential hopeful Barack Obama in West Hollywood, Calif., in June 2008.

gay and lesbian Americans should be treated fairly and equally," Obama said from the White House. "At a certain point, I've just concluded that, for me personally, it is important for me to go ahead and affirm that: I think same-sex couples should be able to get married."

Election-Year Motivation?

When Obama broke onto the scene with a vaunted speech at the Democrats' 2004 convention in Boston, support for gay marriage from a major-party presidential candidate was unthinkable. During that election, Democratic nominee John Kerry opposed same-sex marriage and instead pushed civil unions—legal agreements that stopped short of marriage in the eyes of government. Four years later, when Obama was the nominee, he, too, opposed same-sex marriage in favor of civil unions. But in that short time, there had been a shift in public opinion, thanks in part to a handful of state-court rulings on the issue, and once Obama entered the White House, it was clear he was far friendlier toward LGBT rights than any of his predecessors.

Through the rearview mirror of cynicism, it was easy to write off Obama's shift as an election-year ploy aimed at courting voters and donors; and if that's what it was, the move certainly seemed to work. While less than 2% of the population identifies as gay, an estimated 1 in 16 of Obama's biggest fundraisers in 2012 were LGBT Americans. And polls found that 76% of voters who identified as gay, lesbian or bisexual supported him that November.

Yet there was more to the move than appeasing potential supporters. Obama had long been uneasy with the stance of opposition to same-sex marriage he had taken in 2008. He had signaled to his advisers that he wanted to level with voters before his final election. The two most influential women in his life, First Lady Michelle Obama and White House counselor Valerie Jarrett, were pushing for the shift, and Obama himself had spoken to friends and staffers who were in same-sex relationships. Privately, his advisers had been meeting with experts across the political spectrum, including an openly gay former Republican National Committee chairman, to help their boss navigate the never-before-spoken position.

Obama had also set the stage for his change of heart through policies he enacted during his first term. Early on, the State Department extended benefits to people traveling with their same-sex partners at embassies abroad, and in 2011, Obama signed the repeal of the "don't ask, don't tell" policy that had barred homosexuals from serving openly in the military. During this same period, his Justice Department also stopped defending the '90s-era Defense of Marriage Act, which defined marriage, from a federal-government perspective, as a union between a man and a woman.

CULTURAL BLOWBACK TO THE MARRIAGE RULING WAS FAST AND FIERCE.

Those moves in turn opened the doors for an inheritance-law case, filed by a gay woman, that made its way to the Supreme Court in 2013. The lawsuit successfully challenged an IRS ruling that a tax exemption did not apply to same-sex unions. In 2015, when the high court issued a separate, historic decision, declaring bans on same-sex marriage unconstitutional, Obama ordered his White House illuminated in the rainbow colors of the LGBT Pride flag.

Obama was buoyed in part by generational politics. He knew that his party was adding scores of new voters as the GOP's official platform stood against same-sex-marriage rights. "When I go to college campuses, sometimes I talk to college Republicans who think that I have terrible policies on the economy or on foreign policy but are very clear that when it comes to same-sex equality or sexual orientation, that they believe in equality," the president said. "You know, Malia and Sasha, they've got friends whose parents are same-sex couples. . . . It wouldn't dawn on them that somehow their friends' parents would be treated differently. It doesn't make sense to them."

Fierce Reaction

The cultural blowback to the marriage ruling was fast and fierce. Foes of the measure rushed forward with religious-liberty laws, which allowed businesses to deny LGBT patrons service under the cover of protecting religious workers' First Amendment rights to practice their faith. Other states offered so-called bathroom bills, which likened transgender individuals to sexual predators and left many Americans uncomfortable with talk about one of the most private rooms in life. Conservative groups continued to push efforts to chip away at LGBT rights. And in 2016 Republicans nominated Indiana governor Mike Pence, a longtime foe of LGBT rights and one of the original governors pushing for religious-liberty laws, as their vice-presidential nominee.

But excluding people from rights and benefits or limiting them has been politically risky in America for decades now, at least at the national level. Republican president Richard Nixon was no fan of the Civil Rights Act that his Democratic predecessor Lyndon Johnson signed into law, but he didn't make scrapping the legislation a priority for his administration. Likewise, President George W. Bush was no fan of Bill Clinton's program that provided health care to poor children, but Bush ended up working with liberal senator Ted Kennedy on a K–12 education overhaul that added help for many of the same kids. And Obama campaigned against a section of a Bush Medicare drug program that created a financial burden on consumers, but during his time in office, Obama never eliminated the provision.

The public has shifted so strongly, so quickly on the issues surrounding LGBT rights that rolling back these advancements would be tough. "Through countless acts of quiet courage, America learned that love has no limits, and marriage equality is now a reality across the land," Obama said, addressing the Democratic National Convention in July 2016. At that event, human-rights activist Sarah McBride became the first transgender person to speak at a major party's nominating convention—another sign of how times have changed in eight years.

THE BIG, WIDE DIVIDE

Instead of the togetherness he sought, Obama faced unified opposition in the capital

By Zeke J. Miller

Barack Obama is not one to get worked up. He was so calm during the intensity and frenzy of the 2008 presidential campaign that he earned the moniker No-Drama Obama, and throughout many years of conflict with the GOP in Congress, he maintained a Spock-like equilibrium. But at a fundraiser for the Democratic National Committee in June 2015, the president of the United States got a little exercised.

"I am frustrated, and you have every right to be frustrated, because Congress doesn't work the way it should," Obama told big-ticket supporters at the DNC event in Beverly Hills, Calif. "Issues are left untended. Folks are more interested in scoring political points than getting things done."

The comments were a far cry from those of 2008's candidate Obama. Carried into office on the slogan "Hope and Change," the Democratic challenger vowed his election would be more than just a rejection of the Bush years: it would represent an opportunity to "fundamentally change the way Washington works." And yet, despite the historically high public approval ratings attending the coda of his tenure, Obama's time in office may go down as one of the most polarizing in the capital's history.

The president delivers his 2015 State of the Union speech.

An Eloquent Trailblazer

In 2007, when Obama, then 45, launched his bid for the White House, he was a transformational leader with a progressive agenda to fit. The first black candidate to mount a serious bid for a major-party nomination, he ran a campaign that galvanized young people and drew a record turnout of minority voters to the polls. During the bitter primary fight, Obama took the delegate lead from insider-favored Hillary Clinton and clinched the nomination in St. Paul in June 2008. His historical position seemed assured, and he was favored to win the general election.

Minutes after making history, Obama took the stage. But the reaction to his closing remarks seemed to foreshadow the troubles that lay ahead: "This was the moment when the rise of the oceans began to slow and our planet began to heal; this was the moment when we ended a war and secured our nation and restored our image as the last, best hope on Earth," he told the crowd, emphasizing the need for a unity of purpose. Obama believed his nomination—and eventual election—could be a turning point in history.

While attendees cheered, GOP insiders seized on the words and mocked them as evidence of a God complex. "Moses made the waters recede, but he had help," economist Irwin Stelzer wrote in a column in the *London Daily Telegraph*.

In the face-off with Republican John McCain, Obama won by the largest margin in two decades, receiving 365 Electoral College votes and 52.9% of the popular vote. But that seemed not to matter once he was sworn in. Almost immediately after taking office in

Mark Barden, left, whose son died in the Newtown school shooting, speaks after the Senate rejected a change to background checks in 2013.

2009, the crushing reality of the job Obama had undertaken set in. With an economy in free fall, two overseas wars and a mandate to carry out sweeping change, the inertia of the nation's capital proved daunting.

Having never run anything larger than a three-dozen-person Senate office, Obama wasn't accustomed to management, and as a Washington neophyte, he lacked the relationships—and the patience—to cajole lawmakers. And it wasn't as if Republicans were waiting for a phone call. From Obama's first day in office, Republicans plotted a path of unified opposition to his every proposal, even those they had supported just months before. From economic stimulus to immigration reform, the door was closed to GOP cooperation. "We thought—correctly, I think—that the only way the American people would know that a great debate was going on was if the measures were not bipartisan," then–Senate minority leader Mitch McConnell told *The Atlantic* in 2011.

Tensions between the parties mounted as the president began seeking support for the Affordable Care Act, the largest reform to the nation's health-care system since Medicaid. The goal was ambitious by any measure, and even Obama's first chief of staff, Rahm Emanuel, counseled him to focus on other priorities, fearing the legislation would be controversial and doom any chances of Obama getting re-elected. Obama's decision to go ahead anyway is now a key component of any retelling of his presidency.

The harsh realities of Washington undermined Obama's brand. Without GOP support, Obama pushed through his historic law, but the struggle forced him to operate as a traditional politician, tarnishing his image and sending his approval ratings spiraling downward.

The fight over what came to be known as Obamacare paralleled the rise of "birtherism," the false claim that Obama was born in Kenya and was therefore ineligible to be the U.S. president. (He was born in Hawaii.) There were also unfounded allegations that he was Muslim. (He is Protestant.) Democrats cast those Republican efforts to stymie Obama in racial terms. Polls showed that large swaths of the GOP base believed those falsehoods anyway, which further pressured their representatives to shun any opportunities to reach agreement with Obama.

The rancor overtook the midterm elections of 2010, and GOP leaders, conservative pundits and Tea Party activists seized the moment to press their advantage. "A significant portion of our party believed Obama was a Kenyan-born, Muslim imposter, and we catered to those votes," said one Republican operative involved in the 2010 campaign. At the ballot box, furious GOP voters and disaffected independents registered their discontent. A wave of moderate Democrats was swept from the Congress, a new crop of purist conservatives was ushered in, and control of the House shifted to the Republicans.

Hope and Change, Redux

As he traveled the country seeking re-election in 2012, Obama rallied supporters to the polls with the reassurance that the "fever will break" with his return to office. But despite another convincing win in the general election, his second swearing-in provided no relief. Congressional deadlock only deepened. Almost immediately Obama recognized that to accomplish anything in his second term, he'd have to go it alone. To work around Congress, he turned to unilateral executive actions, a stunning reversal for a president who had railed against his predecessor for resorting to the same maneuvers.

The battles piled up. Enraged by the executive actions, the Republicans filed lawsuit after lawsuit to stop them. There was a showdown over the debt ceiling, which shut down the government and prompted the first-ever cut in the nation's credit rating. Legislating froze. In the aftermath of the December 2012 Newtown school shooting, Democrats introduced a gun-control bill, but it was defeated by the GOP, prompting Obama to lash out: "The gun lobby and its allies willfully lied about the bill," he said from the Rose Garden. The divisiveness of that debate quickly scuttled hopes for a bipartisan immigration-reform bill.

The realities of running the massive federal bureaucracy caught up with Obama as he prepared to launch Healthcare.gov, through which millions of Americans would need to subscribe for health insurance coverage under Obamacare. The website rollout was a boondoggle of epic proportions, with technological mismanagement undercutting the notion that his tech-forward politics could solve all problems. It also furthered the divide between the Affordable Care Act's supporters and opponents.

Some say Obama contributed to the popularity of Donald Trump, whose rise to the presidency fed off the feeling of persistent gridlock that Obama, through his words of indignation, helped foster. Trump's doom-and-gloom vision of America was crafted to oppose Obama's optimism, and his views tapped into an increasingly frustrated and vocal slice of the American electorate. "But for Barack Obama, Donald Trump's effect would not be nearly as strong as it is," Jeb Bush said in December 2015. Obama allies prefer to focus on the GOP's obstruction. "They encouraged the worst instincts of the Tea Party and made promises they couldn't deliver on, like Obama repealing the law with his name in it," said one White House veteran.

For his part, Obama adjusted the timeline on his lofty pledge to reform the nation's politics. "It takes decades of work sometimes just to make a little bit of progress," Obama said at a 2015 fundraiser of changing the broken political system. "Sometimes," he went on, "it takes a century to make a little bit of progress."

SOCIAL-MEDIA MASTER

In the era of hashtags, tweets and quirky videos, Obama proved a deft communicator in chief

By Tessa Berenson

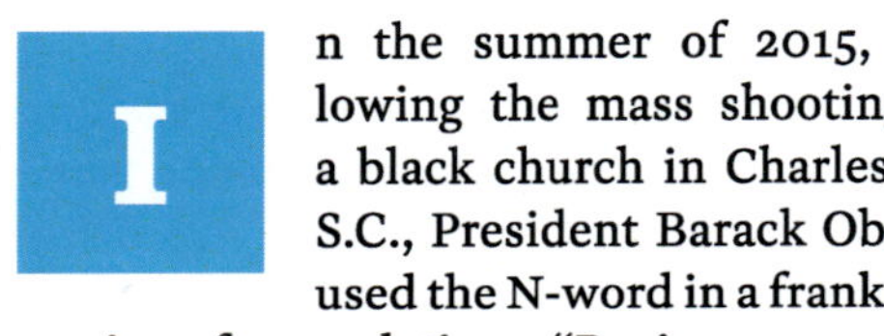

In the summer of 2015, following the mass shooting at a black church in Charleston, S.C., President Barack Obama used the N-word in a frank discussion of race relations. "Racism, we are not cured of. And it's not just a matter of it not being polite to say 'n-----' in public," Obama remarked in comments that reverberated across the nation.

Yet America's first black president had not said the word in an address broadcast on the networks or even on the capital's cable favorite, C-SPAN. Instead, he had gone one-on-one with Marc Maron, a comic turned podcast host who records *WTF with Marc Maron* from a garage in Los Angeles. "I cried a little bit because it was just so overwhelming," an emotional Maron told listeners in the next episode of the show.

Reaching the American public via press conference can seem so analog. In this syncopated era of 24/7 news, Twitter, Snapchat, Facebook, Instagram, webcasts and digital downloads, President Obama has charted a new communications path for the commander in chief. He has deployed hashtags to execute political messaging and quirky videos to sway public opinion. To rally support for the Affordable Care Act, the president appeared on *Between Two Ferns*, an online comedy program hosted by Zach Galifianakis. To inform millennials about the Iran nuclear deal, he turned to the upstart news site Mic. His office logged on to Facebook to announce sentence commutations for low-level prisoners and posted on his Instagram to promote climate-change awareness.

The of-the-moment media strategy satisfied multiple beasts. It showed that a president with academic tendencies also had a funny bone, allowed Obama to communicate directly with the electorate and fostered a more brash, contemporary-style interaction with the public. Viral culture, remember, is anything but Tom Brokaw–respectful.

More subtly, direct posting allowed the president to sidestep probing journalists, says Scott Talan, an assistant professor at American University's School of Communication: "There's not a lot of hard questions or back-and-forth. It's sort of like showing a

Obama records an episode of the podcast *WTF with Marc Maron* in 2015, top; appears in 2014 on the talk show *Between Two Ferns* with Zach Galifianakis, near right; and, in 2015, horses around with Jerry Seinfeld for the Web series *Comedians in Cars Getting Coffee*.

little bit behind the Wizard of Oz—'Hey, I'm just a person, and this is personal'—and yet it removes a lot of the scrutiny and the in-depth analysis."

A Man of His Moment

Given the times we live in, you could say the presidential embrace of social media was inevitable. During Obama's two terms, traditional news outlets withered as blogging and selfies took off. Twitter was founded in 2006, less than three years before Obama took office; Instagram was launched almost two years into his first term. When Obama started his administration, he employed just a handful of "new media" staffers; he exits with an approximately 20-person unit, including teams for video, design, product, content and social media.

"No longer is it that the president of the United States stands on a podium, delivers remarks, and every network covers it, every major newspaper covers it, and those are the only places where people get their information," says Jen Psaki, the White House communications director for Obama since 2015. "The bully pulpit is dead."

A BUZZFEED VIDEO IN WHICH OBAMA MUGGED FOR THE CAMERA WAS VIEWED MORE THAN 15 MILLION TIMES.

Obama arrived in the White House with considerable social-media savvy. One of his key advisers for the 2008 presidential campaign, dubbed "the Facebook election," was Chris Hughes, a co-founder of the social network. Spearheading Obama's new-media strategy, Hughes created a grassroots online community platform that allowed supporters to self-organize and devised an outlet so the public could donate small dollar amounts online. The campaign of Obama's Republican opponent, John McCain, also tapped social networks, though less effectively. That year, 66% of people under age 30 voted for Obama, the largest gap between young voters and other age groups than in any presidential election since exit polling began in 1972, according to Pew research. About half of voters over 30 voted for him.

Keeping Up the Pace

Once he settled in, Obama was quick to fortify his digital-media game. The White House blogged, shot its own photos and video, and distributed the material through sites like Flickr. For Obama's first State of the Union address in 2010, aides set up ways to receive and answer questions from the public on the video-sharing site YouTube and also Google. In 2011 Obama staged a White House "Twitter town hall," moderated by the site's co-founder Jack Dorsey.

The experiments seemed to pay off. After the president made that Affordable Care Act pitch on *Between Two Ferns* in 2014, traffic on the ACA enrollment website spiked by 32,000 visits, according to Healthcare.gov. In 2015, to remind the public that the annual deadline for enrolling in the program was approaching, Obama shot a video with BuzzFeed in which he used a selfie stick and made silly faces in a mirror. The video was viewed more than 15 million times in its first eight hours on YouTube. "[The purpose] is not to generate viral videos about fun and light topics," says Psaki. "It's just a different way of using the tools that are at our disposal."

Still, sometimes it really was just about the laughs. When Obama appeared on Jerry Seinfeld's Web series *Comedians in Cars Getting Coffee* in 2015, the two men discussed topics such as Obama's underwear preference (all the same brand and same color) and favorite snack (nachos) without broaching any serious political topics. Seated behind the wheel of a 1963 Corvette Stingray split-window coupe, Obama was visibly tickled. "I'm appreciably cooler than I was just two minutes ago," he told Seinfeld.

As he exits the White House, Obama leaves a road map so that his successors might be even cooler—and even more digitally adept. "He's grown and was there in some ways as the perfect president for this new communication ecosystem," says Talan. "I think other presidents will follow his lead."

Keegan-Michael Key translates for Obama at the 2015 dinner.

COMIC RELIEF

You need a few jokes to get through eight years in Washington, and Obama delivered some zingers at the Correspondents' Dinner

By Courtney Mifsud

Sometimes called "nerd prom" for the roster of journalists, Hill staffers, A-list policy wonks and Hollywood types who attend, the annual White House Correspondents' Dinner is a hot-ticket event for Washington insiders every spring. The evening kicks off with the president delivering a joke-filled speech, followed by a comedian who roasts the commander in chief, plus figures inside and outside the Beltway. President Obama was a natural behind the lectern, often funnier than the professional comic. In his eight appearances, he lightly teased his daughters, Sasha and Malia, skewered Fox News and made fun of Donald Trump. Here are some highlights.

2009

"Now, Sasha and Malia aren't here tonight because they're grounded. You can't just take Air Force One on a joyride to Manhattan. I don't care whose kids you are."

2010

"It's been quite a year since I've spoken here last—lots of ups, lots of downs—except for my approval ratings, which have just gone down. But that's politics. It doesn't bother me. Besides, I happen to know that my approval ratings are still very high in the country of my birth."

"A few weeks ago I was able to throw out the first pitch at the Nationals game. And I don't know if you saw it, but I threw it a little high and a little outside. This is how Fox News covered it: 'President panders to extreme left wing of batter box.' "

2011

"As some of you heard, the state of Hawaii released my official long-form birth certificate. Hopefully this puts all doubts to rest. But just in case there are any lingering questions, tonight I'm prepared to go a step further. Tonight, for the first time, I am releasing my official birth video. Now, I warn you—no one has seen this footage in 50 years, not even me. But let's take a look. *[A clip from* The Lion King *plays.]* Oh, well. Back to square one. I want to make clear to the Fox News table: That was a joke."

2012

"In 2009, I took office in the face of some enormous challenges. Now, some have said I blame too many problems on my predecessor, but let's not forget that's a practice that was initiated by George W. Bush. Since then, Congress and I have certainly had our differences, yet I've tried to be civil, to not take any cheap shots. And that's why I want to especially thank all the members who took a break from their exhausting schedule of not passing any laws to be here tonight."

2013

"I had dinner with a number of the Republican senators. And I'll admit it wasn't easy. I proposed a toast—it died in committee."

2014

"Let's face it, Fox, you'll miss me when I'm gone. It will be harder to convince the American people that Hillary was born in Kenya."

2015

"After the midterm elections, my advisers asked me, 'Mr. President, do you have a bucket list?' And I said, 'Well, I have something that rhymes with "bucket list." ' Take executive action on immigration? Bucket. New climate regulations? Bucket."

Obama also brought in actor and comedian Keegan-Michael Key as Luther, his "anger translator," who took the president's polite and pragmatic comments and expressed how he really felt in comments like this:

LUTHER: Oh, and CNN, thank you so much for the wall-to-wall Ebola coverage. For two whole weeks, we were one step away from *The Walking Dead*.

2016

"I love Joe Biden, I really do. And I want to thank him for his friendship, for his counsel, for always giving it to me straight, for not shooting anybody in the face. Thank you, Joe."

"And there's one area where Donald [Trump]'s experience could be invaluable—and that's closing Guantánamo. Because Trump knows a thing or two about running waterfront properties into the ground."

THE POWER OF MICHELLE

As "mom in chief," the First Lady championed kids and healthy eating and reveled in a Beaver Cleaver family life

By Jay Newton-Small

Michelle Obama's address to the Democratic National Convention in July 2016 was as classy as it was classic. To an adoring crowd, the First Lady painted both a positive vision of America and a personal one, discussing the challenge of guiding two young daughters during eight years in the White House. Without mentioning Donald Trump by name, Michelle made clear how she and her family are so fundamentally different from the GOP nominee.

"How we insist that the hateful language they hear from public figures on TV does not represent the true spirit of this country. How we explain that when someone is cruel or acts like a bully, you don't stoop to their level," the First Lady told a rapt audience. "No, our motto is, when they go low, we go high."

The speech not only won Michelle even more praise than the address delivered by her husband two nights later, it raised a question with audiences across the country: If former First Lady Hillary Clinton is the 2016 Democratic nominee for president, could Michelle Obama one day earn such an opportunity?

It was a remarkable moment. Many forget that going into the general election in 2008, Michelle was seen at times as a potential liability for Barack Obama. Her speeches could sound stark and stern compared with her husband's roof raisers. In South Carolina, she talked bleakly about America being "just downright mean" and how the lives of most people in recent years had "gotten progressively worse." Before the Wisconsin primary in February 2008, she famously remarked that "for the first time in my adult lifetime, I am really proud of my country." Though both Obamas tried to explain that Michelle meant she was proud to see so many people turning out to vote, the comment drew a firestorm of criticism. The *National Review*, a conservative publication, dubbed her "Mrs. Grievance" and described her as bitter and anti-American.

Yet Michelle managed to rise above. By the time she held the Bible for her husband on Inauguration Day, her approval rating had jumped to 68%. And she was just getting started. The First Lady tackled obesity in America with her "Let's Move!" program and her emphasis on healthy eating. She overhauled school lunches, stripping soda and candy machines from schools. She became a trendsetter. Clothes she wore flew off the shelves. Animal breeders couldn't keep up

The First Lady pauses before delivering her speech at the Democratic National Convention in 2016.

MICHELLE

with the demand for Portuguese water dogs after Bo, and later Sunny, joined the family. In 2009—for whatever it's worth—Michelle became the first First Lady to make *Maxim*'s hottest-women-in-the-world list.

In a League of Her Own

Of all the people given credit for propelling Barack Obama into the Oval Office, none had a greater impact than his wife. In the Obama world, not only was she Barack's resolute and loyal "rock," but her contacts were invaluable, some say essential, to her husband's ascent from the Illinois state senate to the U.S. Senate to the White House.

A Chicago native, Michelle Robinson had deep roots in the city's South Side. She went to high school with Santita Jackson, Rev. Jesse Jackson's daughter, and early on forged ties with Jackson's powerful civil rights group, Rainbow Push. As an aide to Mayor Richard Daley in the early 1990s, she gained access for her husband to Chicago's political class. Her later community-outreach work helped Obama establish a network of young activists in the city. "Her being from Chicago, from the South Side of Chicago, was an asset to Barack in terms of enhancing his ties to the community," says Valerie Jarrett, Michelle's boss in the Daley administration who became an adviser to Obama in the White House.

Barack and Michelle met while working at a corporate-law firm in the summer of 1989. Obama was an intern at Sidley Austin, a prestigious Chicago law practice that also happened to employ Robinson, a young intellectual-property lawyer and Harvard Law School graduate. Obama kept asking Robinson out, but she was leery of an office romance. Eventually Obama prevailed—their first date was to see Spike Lee's *Do the Right Thing*—and within a year the couple were engaged.

Although Sidley Austin partners may have expected Obama to turn down a job offer to pursue public service, Michelle's family and friends were surprised when she made a similar decision, giving up her corporate-law salary to work for Mayor Daley. "I'm sure at Sidley she made more money than her parents ever made," her college roommate Angela Acree said. "It just seemed incredible at the time that she'd leave."

Yet the transition appeared seamless. While Barack taught at the University of Chicago Law School and dove into voter-registration drives, Michelle thrived in the nonprofit and education sectors. She left the Daley administration to head up the Chicago office of a new charity that was forming, Public Allies, which helped place young people at nonprofits. Later, as associate dean of student services at the University of Chicago, she launched a community-service program for undergraduates; she then moved to the university's medical school to work in a struggling Hyde Park neighborhood.

One sometimes sore point was home life. The child of a stay-at-home mother and a city pump operator, Michelle had grown up in a close-knit family that ate every meal together, played Monopoly and read together. Even though she was working full time, Michelle wanted her daughters, Malia, born in 1998, and

The First Lady at Winfield House in London, 2011, left; her initiatives included encouraging exercise and healthy eating, above.

Sasha, born in 2001, to have a childhood similar to her own. That became increasingly difficult as Barack commuted first to Springfield as an Illinois state senator and then to Washington, D.C., after he was elected to the U.S. Senate. "My wife's anger toward me seemed barely contained," Obama wrote in his autobiography *The Audacity of Hope*. " 'You only think about yourself,' she would tell me. 'I never thought I'd have to raise a family alone.' "

It was not until the next stage of her life that Michelle finally got to be a stay-at-home mom like her mother. That home, of course, was the White House.

Making the White House Her Stage

Many speculated on what kind of First Lady Michelle Obama might be: an activist like Eleanor Roosevelt or a traditionalist like Laura Bush. Would she have an office in the West Wing, as Hillary Clinton did during her husband's administration? Instead, she threw herself into the role of "mom in chief," reveling in a Beaver Cleaver family life and putting her very distinctive stamp on the White House and its operations. Under the new FLOTUS, 1600 Pennsylvania Avenue became looser and more fun. Michelle colored a fountain green for St. Patrick's Day, mixed the Woodrow Wilson china with the World's Fair glasses at a state dinner and installed beehives and a kitchen garden on the South Lawn.

Michelle also tried to make the White House a presence throughout the Washington community. She dispatched role models to schools across the district, including singers Alicia Keys and Sheryl Crow; Ann Dunwoody, the first female four-star general; and Mae Jemison, the first female African-American astronaut. Michelle herself visited the violence-ridden Anacostia High School, where signs alert students to the supplies available through the Baby Bonus Bucks Redemption Program. She spoke with them about their potential and tried to relate her teen years to theirs. She talked about growing up close to the University of Chicago but never setting foot inside. "It was a fancy college, and it didn't have anything to do with me." Maybe you feel the same way about the White House, she suggested to the students.

As the First Lady's time at 1600 Pennsylvania Avenue comes to an end, it in fact appears quite unlikely that she would consider a run for the White House herself—her stinging rebuke of Donald Trump for bragging about sexually assaulting women and the appearance of HILLARY 2016 MICHELLE 2024 bumper stickers notwithstanding. "Let me tell you that there are three things that are certain in life," Barack Obama told a town hall in Baton Rouge, La., in January 2016. "Death. Taxes. And Michelle is not running for president."

Two months later, Michelle reiterated that point at the interactive media and music conference South by Southwest, citing her daughters as reasons. Besides, she added, "You don't have to be president of the United States to do wonderful, marvelous things."

ADVICE AND CONSENT

The influencers and strategists who had the president's ear

Timothy Geithner

Secretary of the Treasury

During 2009's economic crisis, Obama weighed two options to stabilize the financial system: punish the banks, as White House political advisers wanted, or test the banks to see if they could survive more turmoil, the course pushed by Geithner. Obama sided with Geithner; when the plan worked, trust followed. Geithner was with the administration until 2013.

Lawrence Summers

Director, National Economic Council

Considered brilliant albeit at times impolitic, Summers was a key Obama adviser during the financial meltdown, and in 2013, he was the president's top pick to replace Ben Bernanke at the Federal Reserve. Summers withdrew his name after various liberal groups protested his attitude, decisions on the economy and insensitivity to women.

Joe Biden

Vice President

The odds certainly were against Joe Biden becoming Barack Obama's de facto adviser in chief. Not only is the former U.S. senator a generation older and the temperamental opposite of the president, but back in 2007, when both men were vying for the Democratic presidential nomination, Biden set off a news firestorm by describing Obama in racially tinged terms. (He later apologized for characterizing Obama as "clean" and "articulate.")

Yet as vice president from 2009 to 2016, Biden evolved into one of the president's top confidants and sounding boards. It was Biden who directed the implementation of Obama's 2009 economic stimulus and who led many of the administration's budget negotiations with congressional leaders. When there was a crisis abroad, Obama often dispatched Biden as his proxy. The two even overcame uncomfortable moments, such as when Biden declared his support for gay marriage, forcing Obama to do the same.

Their personal relationship deepened, too. After the vice president's son Beau had a stroke and Biden worried about supporting the younger man's family, Obama offered to give his second-in-command money so he would not have to sell his home. The media, which typically delight in exposing frayed relationships between presidents and their deputies, fell head over heels for the bromance, with *The Atlantic* even asking if Biden was "The Most Influential Vice President in History." Time, of course, will tell. But on Obama's 55th birthday, there was this: a tweet from Biden to Obama, with an image of intertwined friendship bracelets with "Joe" and "Barack" spelled out in beads. The message gushed, "Happy 55th, Barack! A brother to me, a best friend forever." The image went viral.

Pete Rouse
Senior Adviser

Obama was a newly elected senator from Illinois in 2004 when he hired Pete Rouse to set up his D.C. office. A well-connected Capitol Hill veteran—Rouse was sometimes called "the 101st senator"—he eventually became Obama's second-longest-serving top aide in the White House, entrusted with staffing, strategy and troubleshooting.

Rahm Emanuel
Chief of Staff

Famously sharp-elbowed and foul-mouthed, Emanuel (now mayor of Chicago) was brought into the Obama inner circle to get things done—and succeeded. As chief of staff over Obama's first 20 months, he helped engineer signature wins, including the economic stimulus package and the bank bailout. Emanuel also influenced some foreign policy.

John Brennan
Director, CIA

Brennan got to know Obama in 2008, when he acted as a security-policy adviser to the candidate's presidential campaign and transition teams. In 2009 he was tapped by Obama to be the administration's counterterrorism expert, a post he used to advocate for the drone war. In 2013, Obama nominated Brennan to be CIA chief.

David Plouffe
Senior Adviser

The obsessive, data-driven operative behind Obama's 2008 victory, Plouffe is also the adviser considered most in tune with the president's personality. When fellow adviser David Axelrod returned to Chicago to help run Obama's re-election campaign, it was Plouffe who stepped into Axelrod's shoes at the White House.

Eric Holder
Attorney General

A chance 2004 dinner-party meeting in Washington, D.C., paid off for Holder, a former judge and prosecutor who became one of the few Washington players in Obama's Chicago-based circle. Holder was part of the advisory committee that picked Sen. Joe Biden as Obama's running mate, and in 2008, Obama nominated him for U.S. attorney general. He stepped down in 2014.

Valerie Jarrett
Senior Adviser

A confidante of the president's since the early 1990s, Jarrett has been called the First Friend and the Obama Whisperer for her unique relationship with POTUS. She has served as the president's social and political middleman, connecting Obama to CEOs and Washington insiders and also advising him on Supreme Court nominations and cabinet picks.

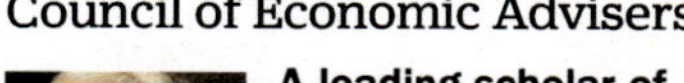

Christina Romer
Council of Economic Advisers

A leading scholar of macroeconomic history and an expert on the Great Depression, Romer was part of the economic SWAT team assembled by president-elect Obama in 2008 to respond to the financial crisis. As chief economist, she was behind the $800 billion economic stimulus package. She returned to the University of California, Berkeley, in 2010.

Denis McDonough
Chief of Staff

After cycling through more chiefs of staff than any other president, Obama found a keeper in McDonough, his former deputy national security adviser. A disciplined workaholic (remarkably like Obama himself), McDonough, who took over the position in 2013, is described as a control freak whose mission is simple: to carry out the boss's orders.

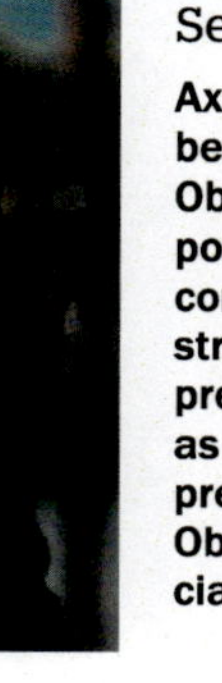

David Axelrod
Senior Adviser

Axelrod, nicknamed Axe, has been perhaps the staunchest Obama believer of all. A former political reporter, the garrulous consultant crafted the media strategy for both of Obama's presidential campaigns and served as official senior adviser to the president from 2009 to 2011 as Obama worked through the financial crisis.

Arne Duncan
Secretary of Education

A founding member of Obama's Chicago circle, Duncan was one of the president's closest cabinet members and, at 6'5", one of his preferred hoops buddies. (The two met on the court in Chicago in the 1990s.) In his seven years as secretary of education, Duncan battled with teachers, the Tea Party and others.

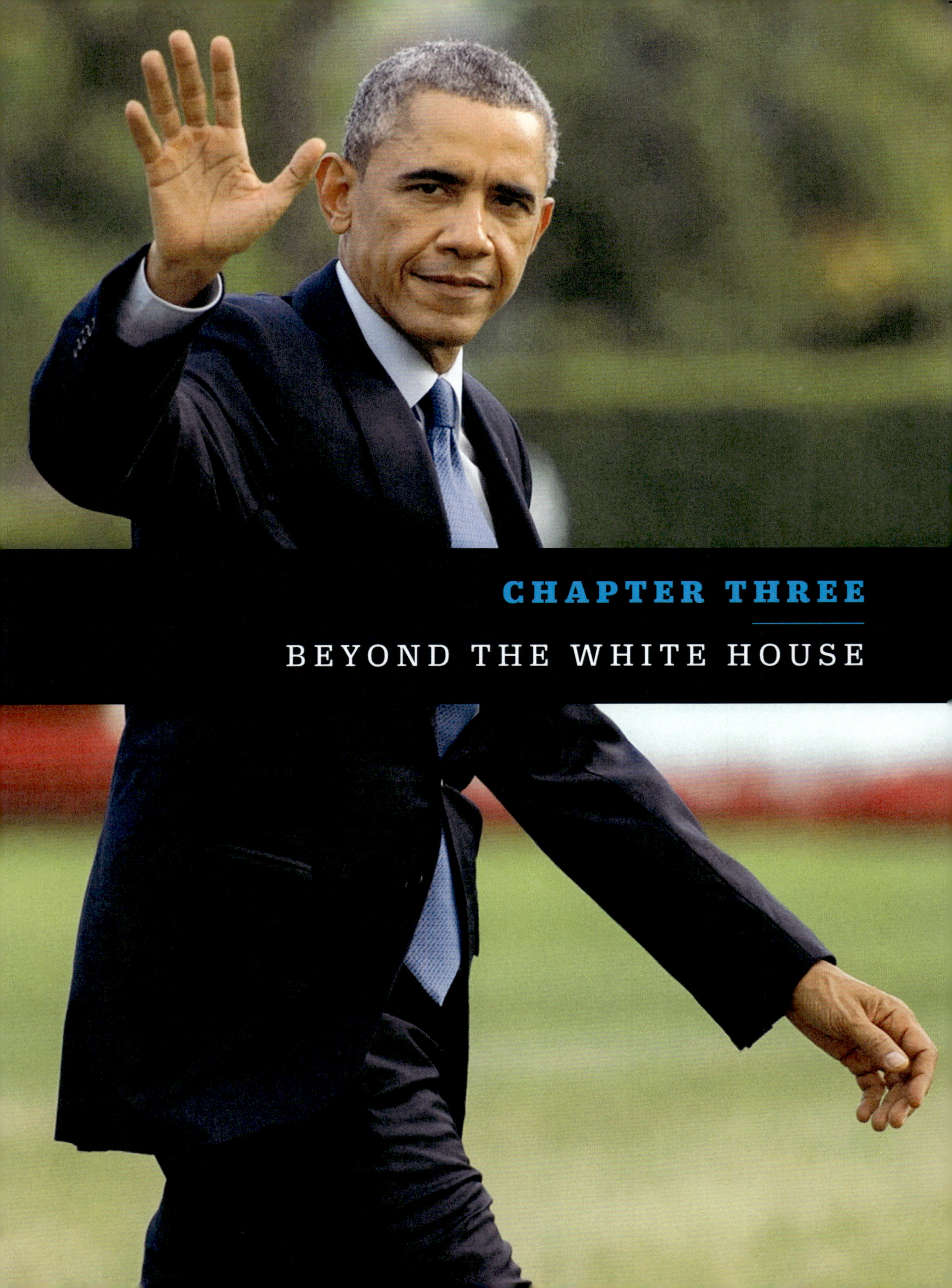

CHAPTER THREE

BEYOND THE WHITE HOUSE

“The future
we want—
opportunity an
security for our
families, a rising
standard of livi
and a sustainab
peaceful planet
for our kids—
all that is withi
our reach.”

—Barack Obama, 2016 State of the Union address

BECOMING CITIZEN OBAMA

The return to civilian life may involve advocacy, the lecture circuit and a whopping book deal

By Zeke J. Miller

Over a late-night martini in the White House's second-floor residence, President Barack Obama has been known to prod his dinner guests with a simple question: What should he do next?

After nearly eight years in the confining bubble of the Oval Office, where a president's most precious asset is time, Obama will soon have an abundance of hours, days and months to forge what he will. So in private dinner parties, often with Silicon Valley executives, Hollywood stars and public intellectuals, the president has kept turning over his guests' ideas: Marshal the cure to a disease. Promote peace abroad. Foster understanding among a diverse society at home.

Obama, at 55, will become one of the youngest ex-presidents in the nation's history, eclipsed by a handful that includes Theodore Roosevelt, Ulysses S. Grant and Bill Clinton. As his time as the leader of the free world comes to a close, Obama is preparing for reentry.

President Obama gazes out onto the South Lawn of the White House during his first year in office.

Switching Gears

The modern post-presidency has been defined by extremes. Bill Clinton launched a high-profile foundation that has had significant impact and has grown exponentially, while also earning many millions of dollars on the speaking circuit. George W. Bush became something of a Texas recluse, making far fewer appearances and taking up watercolor painting. Obama appears ready to chart a course somewhere in between, toggling between the limelight and a return to the social-justice issues that sparked his interest in public service back in the 1980s.

In a notable departure from precedent, Obama and his family will stay in Washington after his term is up so that his daughter Sasha can graduate from her high school, which she is scheduled to do in 2019. The Obamas will live in the Kalorama neighborhood and will become the first First Family to remain in the capital since Woodrow Wilson was president. While the 44th president will surely do his best to give the 45th a free lane to govern, the mere fact that Obama will be in Washington means his comings and goings will very likely be closely chronicled, whether he is out walking the family's dogs, Bo and Sunny, or addressing a policy group.

Given his huge popularity—Obama is exiting with ratings that fall just shy of those of Bill Clinton, who left office in the midst of an economic boom—the ex-president will be a "get" on the speaking circuit, where, if his immediate predecessors are any guide, he has the potential to earn tens of millions of dollars. Already a three-time author, Obama is expected to write a memoir, which could fetch an advance rivaling Bill Clinton's reported $15 million. And despite persistent rumors that the former law professor was open to a Supreme Court nomination, aides say Obama stands by a 2014 statement ruling out the "monastic" lifestyle associated with a seat on the high court.

The return to civilian life will also be a time for Obama to burnish his legacy, as is standard for ex-presidents. George W. Bush launched an institute focused on veterans outreach, expanding health care in Africa and empowering female leaders across the globe. The Clinton Foundation has morphed into a billion-dollar behemoth with health-care, education, climate and global-development arms.

Obama has already kick-started the Obama Foundation, which will take the lead in constructing Obama's presidential library in Chicago as well as the programs that will emanate from it. Longtime Obama friend Marty Nesbitt is overseeing the organization, whose board includes top donors and political advisers. Obama aides are reluctant to discuss initial plans for the organization, arguing that they don't want to distract from his final days in office. But they say tentative ideas include sections devoted to continuing advocacy for Obama's Affordable Care Act and climate-change efforts, both signature items of his presidency. The foundation will also seek to defend Obama's foreign-policy record, including a rapprochement with Cuba and the Iran nuclear deal.

Exploring Racial Issues

Another topic that America is likely to hear more about from citizen Obama is the complex interaction between racial tension, gun control and criminal-justice reform. Although he made history as the first black president, and racial identity was the basis of his best-selling autobiography *Dreams from My Father*, Obama was wary of discussing race during much of his tenure in the White House.

That attitude began to change with the 2013 acquittal of George Zimmerman, the neighborhood-watch guard who killed the unarmed black teen Trayvon Martin. The episode struck a chord with Obama, prompting him to open up about the state of the country's race relations. In a televised press conference following Zimmerman's acquittal, the president described the experiences of being followed while shopping in a department store and of hearing the locks engage on car doors as he walked down the street. "Trayvon Martin could have been me 35 years ago," Obama told America.

During the remainder of his second administration, as shootings of black men by police received more attention, Obama began

Clockwise from top left: Participants in an event for My Brother's Keeper meet with the president in 2014; Obama with his family in California in 2016; a mural of Obama in Chicago, 2015

speaking out more frequently about systemic racism and the tension between police and the communities they serve. He is likely to be even more vocal once he leaves office. "These are issues that in a lot of ways have defined his presidency and are unfinished," says one White House official.

Already, Obama has close ties to two nonprofits that could help. In 2014, in the aftermath of the Martin killing, Obama kicked off My Brother's Keeper, a White House initiative advocating mentorship for young men of color that became a stand-alone organization. Obama took on his own group of mentees, mostly black and Hispanic high school students from the Washington area. The president is planning to assume a substantial role in the organization once he is freed from the fundraising restraints and general responsibilities of the White House.

There's also Organizing for Action, a grassroots effort formed from the president's 2012 re-election team to support his legislative agenda. The president has held a steady stream of fundraising events for the nonprofit, which focuses on such matters as climate change and immigration reform. Obama is expected to take on a more formal role with the group after he leaves the White House.

The two organizations help bring Obama full circle to what got him started in public service. "I'll go back to doing the kinds of work that I was doing before, just trying to find ways to help people—help young people get educations, and help people get jobs, and try to bring businesses into neighborhoods that don't have enough businesses," Obama told a group of students in Washington in 2015. "That's the kind of work that I really love to do."

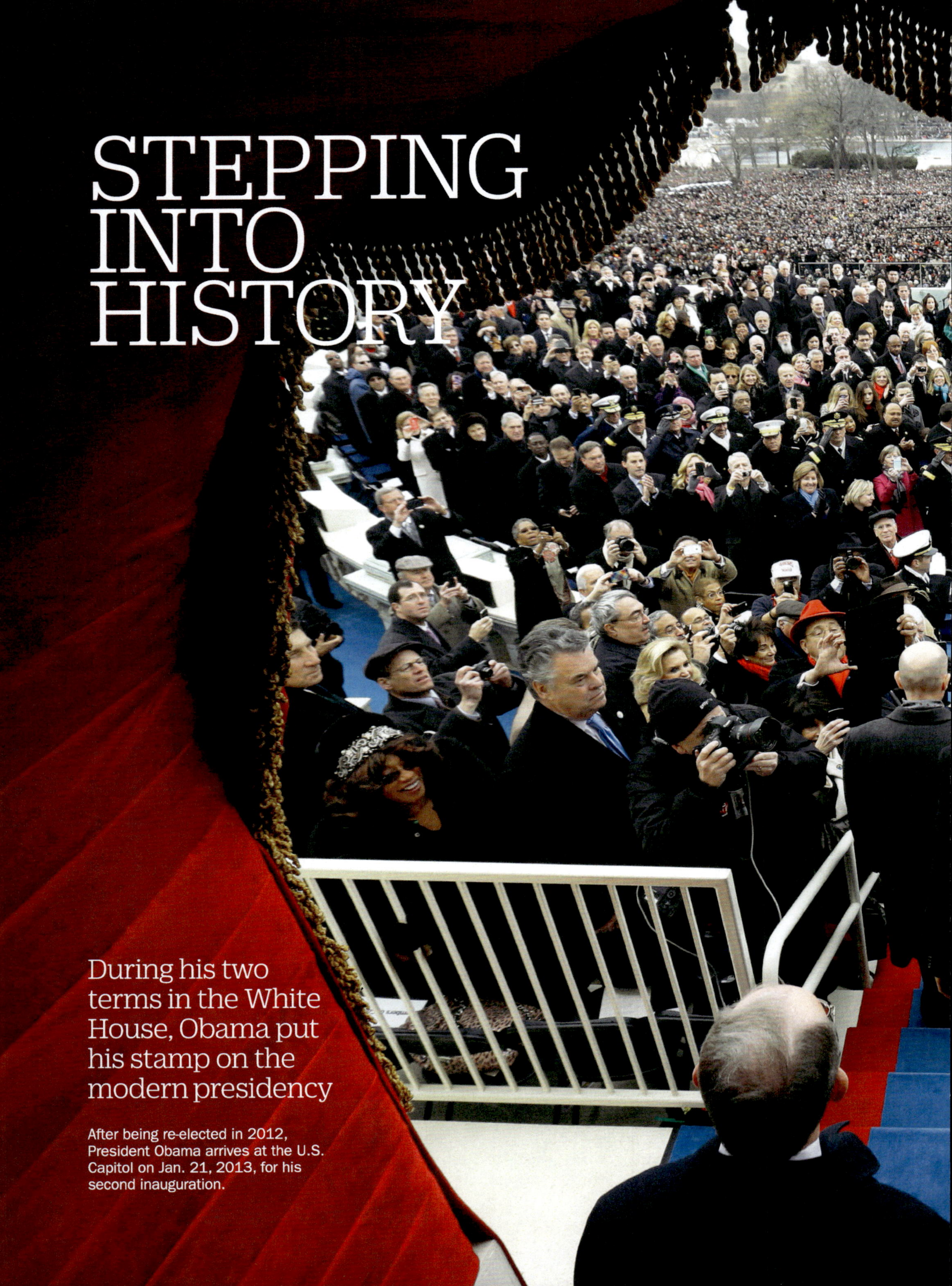

STEPPING INTO HISTORY

During his two terms in the White House, Obama put his stamp on the modern presidency

After being re-elected in 2012, President Obama arrives at the U.S. Capitol on Jan. 21, 2013, for his second inauguration.

Members of Congress

President-elect Obama, his wife Michelle and daughters Malia and Sasha wave to the crowd in Chicago's Grant Park on election night, 2008.

Chicago city officials estimated the size of the crowd in Grant Park on election night in 2008 to be about 240,000 people.

OBAMA
BIDEN

The president pretends to be caught in Spider-Man's web after greeting Halloween trick-or-treater Nicholas Tamarin, the son of a White House aide, in 2012.

Leaders take a break from the 2012 G8 summit to watch soccer. Standing, from left, are the U.K.'s David Cameron, Obama, Germany's Angela Merkel and Jose Manuel Barroso, president of the European Commission.

Some cabinet secretaries and members of Congress join President Obama for a basketball game on the White House court in 2009.

KING'S
COLLEGE

Chief of Staff Denis McDonough, left, and Miguel Rodriguez, director of legislative affairs, share a laugh with the president in the Oval Office in 2013.

After his 2009 inauguration, a long day that included a parade and 10 balls, the new president takes an elevator up to the private residence.

TIME

Editor Nancy Gibbs
Creative Director D.W. Pine
Director of Photography Kira Pollack

BARACK OBAMA: EIGHT YEARS

Editors Kostya Kennedy, Eileen Daspin
Designer D.W. Pine
Photo Editor Patricia Cadley
Writers Graham Allison, Tessa Berenson, Haley Sweetland Edwards, Philip Elliott, Courtney Mifsud, Zeke J. Miller, Jay Newton-Small, Kate Pickert, Maya Rhodan, Mark Thompson, David Von Drehle
Copy Editor Joseph McCombs
Reporter Elizabeth L. Bland
Editorial Production David Sloan

TIME INC. BOOKS
Publisher Margot Schupf
Associate Publisher Allison Devlin
Vice President, Finance Terri Lombardi
Vice President, Marketing Jeremy Biloon
Executive Director, Marketing Services Carol Pittard
Director, Brand Marketing Jean Kennedy
Sales Director Christy Crowley
Assistant General Counsel Andrew Goldberg
Assistant Director, Production Susan Chodakiewicz
Senior Manager, Category Marketing Bryan Christian
Brand Manager Katherine Barnet
Associate Prepress Manager Alex Voznesenskiy
Project Manager Hillary Leary

Editorial Director Kostya Kennedy
Creative Director Gary Stewart
Director of Photography Christina Lieberman
Editorial Operations Director Jamie Roth Major
Senior Editor Alyssa Smith
Associate Art Director Allie Adams
Assistant Art Director Anne-Michelle Gallero
Copy Chief Rina Bander
Assistant Managing Editor Gina Scauzillo
Assistant Editor Courtney Mifsud
Special thanks: Nicole Fisher, Melissa Frankenberry, Kristina Jutzi, Simon Keeble, Seniqua Koger, Kate Roncinske, Kristen Zwicker

Published by Time Books, an imprint of Time Inc. Books
225 Liberty Street · New York, NY 10281

We welcome your comments and suggestions about Time Books. Please write to us at: Time Books, Attention: Book Editors, P.O. Box 62310, Tampa, FL 33662-2310. If you would like to order any of our hardcover Collector's Edition books, please call us at 800-327-6388, Monday through Friday, 7 a.m.–9 p.m. Central Time.

CREDITS

FRONT COVER
Kwaku Alston/Contour by Getty Images

BACK COVER
Pete Souza/The White House

CONTENTS
2 Inez & Vinhoodh/Trunk Archive

PHOTO SWEEP
4 Brooks Kraft LLC/Corbis via Getty Images **6–9** Pete Souza/The White House (2) **10** Doug Mills/The New York Times/Redux

INTRODUCTION
13 Jewel Samad/AFP/Getty Images **14** Samantha Appleton/The White House **15–21** Pete Souza/The White House (4)

A DISTINCTIVE AGENDA
22 Mandel Ngan/AFP/Getty Images **25** Stephen Crowley/The New York Times/Redux **26** (left) Jewel Samad/AFP/Getty Images; Chris Hondros/Getty Images **27** Pete Souza/The White House via Getty Images **31** Lucy Nicholson/Reuters **32** Charles Dharapak/AP Images **34–35** (left to right, top to bottom) Doug Mills/The New York Times/Redux; Nicolas Asfouri/AFP/Getty Images; Pete Souza/The White House; United Nation Relief and Works Agency via Getty Images; ROTA/Camera Press/Redux; Xinhua News Agency/Getty Images; Karwai Tang/WireImage/Getty Images; Jewel Samad/AFP/Getty Images; Cole Burston/Bloomberg via Getty Images; Pete Souza/The White House; Wathiq Khuzaie/Getty Images; Cheriss May/NurPhoto via Getty Images; Saul Loeb/AFP/Getty Images **36** Pete Souza/The White House **38** Scott Peterson/Getty Images **40** Doug Mills/The New York Times/Redux **43** Pete Souza/The White House/MCT via Getty Images **45** Graphic for TIME by Lon Tweeten **47** (from top) Asif Hassan/AFP/Getty Images; Stephen D. Schester/U.S. Air Force via Getty Images; Thomas Janisch/Moment Editorial/Getty Images

HISTORY IN THE MAKING
48 Lawrence Jackson/The White House **50** Doug Mills/The New York Times/Redux **52** (top) Saul Loeb/AFP/Getty Images; David McNew/Getty Images **53** Joe Raedle/Getty Images **54** Callie Shell/Aurora Photos **56** Michael Reynolds/EPA/Redux **58** David McNew/Getty Images **60** Astrid Riecken/EPA/Redux **62** Michael Reynolds/EPA/Redux **65** Pete Souza/The White House (3) **67** Olivier Douliery/White House Pool/ISP Pool Images/Corbis/VCG via Getty Images **69** Aaron P. Bernstein/Getty Images **70** Yui Mok-WPA Pool/Getty Images **71** (top) Amanda Lucidon/The White House; Chuck Kennedy/The White House **72** (from top) Pete Souza/The White House; Vallery Jean/FilmMagic/Getty Images; Susana Gonzalez/Bloomberg via Getty Images **73** (left to right, top to bottom) Joshua Roberts/Bloomberg via Getty Images; Larry Busacca/Getty Images for New York Times; Chip Somodevilla/Getty Images; Joshua Lott/Getty Images; Drew Angerer/Bloomberg via Getty Images; Mandel Ngan/AFP/Getty Images; Brooks Kraft LLC/Corbis via Getty Images; William B. Plowman/NBC/NBC NewsWire via Getty Images; William B. Plowman/NBC NewsWire via Getty Images; Andrew Burton/Getty Images

BEYOND THE WHITE HOUSE
74 Jim Watson/AFP/Getty Images **76** Pete Souza/The White House **78** (top) Pete Souza/The White House; Matt McClain/The Washington Post via Getty Images **79** Brendan Smialowski/AFP/Getty Images **80** Evan Vucci-Pool/Getty Images **82–85** Brooks Kraft LLC/Corbis via Getty Images **86** Pete Souza/The White House via Getty Images **88–95** Pete Souza/The White House (5) **96** (video grab) Courtesy of The White House

TIME AUGMENTED REALITY (AR) EXPERIENCE IMAGE CREDITS
Front Cover (video) Getty Images editorial footage; (still photos in order of appearance) Scott Olson/Getty Images; Michal Czerwonka/Getty Images; Phil Velasquez/Chicago Tribune/MCT via Getty Images; Saul Loeb/AFP/Getty Images; Tasos Katopodis/Getty Images; Joe Raedle/Getty Images; Saul Loeb/AFP/Getty Images; Joe Raedle/Getty Images; Michal Czerwonka/Getty Images (2); Joe Raedle/Getty Images; Chris McGrath/Getty Images; Brooks Kraft LLC/Corbis via Getty Images (2) **43, 53, 96** Video clips courtesy of The White House

OBAMA OUT!

He held his own with Jimmy Fallon on *The Tonight Show*, slow-jamming the news with a straight face. He poked fun at himself (and his dad jeans) reading mean tweets on *Jimmy Kimmel Live*. And at his final White House Correspondents' Dinner roast, President Obama was less controversial but wittier than Larry Wilmore, the pro brought in to entertain the crowd. Among the celebrities on hand were actors Will Smith, Emma Watson and Helen Mirren. But the president's best line was a nod to a star who was not in the room: Los Angeles Lakers basketball player Kobe Bryant, nicknamed "Black Mamba." Fifteen days earlier, Bryant had retired from a 20-year career with a speech to his fans. He put two fingers to his lips, waved goodbye, and said "Mamba out." Obama's dinner exit? He finished his remarks to the guests, put two fingers to his lips, declared "Obama out," and dropped the mic.

▲

This photo leads to an augmented-reality experience through the Time Inc. Special Edition App.

See the Contents page for details. Then point the camera of your phone or tablet to capture the photo above.

44449385R00055

Made in the USA
San Bernardino, CA
15 January 2017